Legal Notice

ISBN-13: 978-1470002312
ISBN-10: 1470002310

D1360500

BOOKS FROM THE GET 800 COLLECTION

28 SAT Math Lessons to Improve Your Score in One Month
    Beginner Course
    Intermediate Course
    Advanced Course

320 SAT Math Problems Arranged by Topic and Difficulty Level

New SAT Math Problems Arranged by Topic and Difficulty Level

320 SAT Math Subject Test Problems Arranged by Topic and Difficulty Level
    Level 1 Test
    Level 2 Test

SAT Prep Book of Advanced Math Problems

The 32 Most Effective SAT Math Strategies

SAT Prep Official Study Guide Math Companion

SAT Vocabulary Book

320 ACT Math Problems Arranged by Topic and Difficulty Level

320 AP Calculus AB Problems Arranged by Topic and Difficulty Level

320 AP Calculus BC Problems Arranged by Topic and Difficulty Level

555 Math IQ Questions for Middle School Students

555 Geometry Problems for High School Students

CONNECT WITH DR. STEVE WARNER

www.facebook.com/SATPrepGet800

www.youtube.com/TheSATMathPrep

www.twitter.com/SATPrepGet800

www.linkedin.com/in/DrSteveWarner

www.pinterest.com/SATPrepGet800

plus.google.com/+SteveWarnerPhD

320 SAT Math Problems arranged
by Topic and Difficulty Level

A Proven Roadmap to
Your First-Choice College

Steve Warner, Ph.D.

Table of Contents

ACTIONS TO COMPLETE BEFORE YOU READ THIS BOOK

1. Purchase a TI-84 or equivalent calculator

It is recommended that you use a TI-84 or comparable calculator for the SAT. Answer explanations in this book will always assume you are using such a calculator.

2. Take a practice SAT from the Official Guide to get your preliminary SAT math score

Use this score to help you determine the problems you should be focusing on (see page 9 for details).

3. Claim your FREE book

Visit the following webpage and enter your email address to receive an electronic copy of the *SAT Prep Official Study Guide Math Companion* for FREE. You will also receive solutions to all the supplemental problems in this book.

www.thesatmathprep.com/320SATprmT1.html

4. 'Like' my Facebook page

This page is updated regularly with SAT prep advice, tips, tricks, strategies, and practice problems. Visit the following webpage and click the 'like' button.

www.facebook.com/SATPrepGet800

INTRODUCTION
THE PROPER WAY TO PREPARE

There are many ways that a student can prepare for the SAT. But not all preparation is created equal. I always teach my students the methods that will give them the maximum result with the minimum amount of effort.

In "The 32 Most Effective SAT Math Strategies" I emphasize the most important techniques for this particular test. That book contains 115 problems that are perfect for implementing the various strategies discussed there. In fact, using that book alone is enough to significantly boost anyone's SAT math score.

The book you are now reading is also self-contained. Each problem was carefully created to ensure that you are making the most effective use of your time while preparing for the SAT. By grouping the problems given here by level and topic I have ensured that you can focus on the types of problems that will be most effective to improving your score.

1. The magical mixture for success

A combination of three components will maximize your SAT math score with the least amount of effort.

- Learning test taking strategies that are specific to the SAT.
- Practicing SAT problems for a small amount of time each day for about three months before the SAT.
- Taking about four practice tests before test day to make sure you are applying the strategies effectively under timed conditions.

I will discuss each of these three components in a bit more detail.

Strategy: The more SAT specific strategies that you know the better off you will be. All the strategies you need to know are in "The 32 Most Effective SAT Math Strategies," as well as 115 problems to practice implementing these strategies. Note that it is not enough to know these strategies. You must practice using them on SAT problems as often as possible.

Practice: The book you are now reading is ideal for accomplishing this task. The problems given in this book are more than enough to vastly improve your current SAT math score. All you need to do is work on these problems for about ten to twenty minutes each day over a period of three to four months and the final result will far exceed your expectations.

Let me further break this component into two subcomponents – **topic** and **level**.

Topic: You want to practice each of the four general math topics given on the SAT and improve in each independently. The four topics are **Number Theory, Algebra and Functions, Geometry,** and **Probability and Statistics.** The problem sets in this book are broken into these four topics.

Level: You will make the best use of your time by primarily practicing problems that are at and slightly above your current ability level. For example, if you are struggling with Level 2 Geometry problems, then it makes no sense at all to practice Level 5 Geometry problems. Keep working on Level 2 until you are comfortable, and then slowly move up to Level 3. Maybe you should never attempt those Level 5 problems. You can get an exceptional score without them (higher than 700).

Tests: You want to take about four practice tests before test day to make sure that you are implementing strategies correctly and using your time wisely under pressure. For this task you should use the second edition of "The Official SAT Study Guide" by the College Board. Take one test every few weeks to make sure that you are implementing all the strategies you have learned correctly under timed conditions. Note that only the second edition has three actual SATs.

2. Practice problems of the appropriate level

Roughly speaking about one third of the math problems on the SAT are easy, one third are medium, and one third are hard. If you answer two thirds of the math questions on the SAT correctly, then your score will be approximately a 600 (out of 800). That's right—you can get about a 600 on the math portion of the SAT without answering a single hard question.

Keep track of your current ability level so that you know the types of problems you should focus on. If you are currently scoring around a 400 on your practice tests, then you should be focusing primarily on Level 1, 2, and 3 problems. You can easily raise your score 100 points without having to practice a single hard problem.

If you are currently scoring about a 500, then your primary focus should be Level 2 and 3, but you should also do some Level 1 and 4 problems.

If you are scoring around a 600, you should be focusing on Level 2, 3, and 4 problems, but you should do some Level 1 and 5 problems as well.

Those of you at the 700 level really need to focus on those Level 4 and 5 problems.

If you really want to refine your studying, then you should keep track of your ability level in each of the four major categories of problems:

- **Number Theory**
- **Algebra and Functions**
- **Probability, Statistics and Data Analysis**
- **Geometry**

For example, many students have trouble with very easy geometry problems, even though they can do more difficult number theory problems. This type of student may want to focus on Level 1, 2, and 3 geometry questions, but Level 3 and 4 number theory questions.

3. Practice in small amounts over a long period of time

Ideally you want to practice doing SAT math problems ten to twenty minutes each day beginning at least 3 months before the exam. You will retain much more of what you study if you study in short bursts than if you try to tackle everything at once.

The only exception is on a day you do a practice test. You should do at least four practice tests before you take the SAT. Ideally you should do your practice tests on a Saturday or Sunday morning. At first you can do just the 3 math sections. The last one or two times you take a practice test you should do the whole test in one sitting. As tedious as this is, it will prepare you for the amount of endurance that it will take to get through this exam.

So try to choose about a twenty minute block of time that you will dedicate to SAT math every night. Make it a habit. The results are well worth this small time commitment.

4. Redo the problems you get wrong over and over and over until you get them right

If you get a problem wrong, and never attempt the problem again, then it is extremely unlikely that you will get a similar problem correct if it appears on the SAT.

Most students will read an explanation of the solution, or have someone explain it to them, and then never look at the problem again. This is *not* how you optimize your SAT score. To be sure that you will get a similar problem correct on the SAT, you must get the problem correct before the SAT—and without actually remembering the problem.

This means that after getting a problem incorrect, you should go over and understand why you got it wrong, wait at least a few days, then attempt the same problem again. If you get it right you can cross it off your list of problems to review. If you get it wrong, keep revisiting it every few days until you get it right. Your score does not improve by getting problems correct. Your score improves when you learn from your mistakes.

5. Check your answers properly

When you go back to check your earlier answers for careless errors *do not* simply look over your work to try to catch a mistake. This is usually a waste of time. Always redo the problem without looking at any of your previous work. Ideally, you want to use a different method than you used the first time.

For example, if you solved the problem by picking numbers the first time, try to solve it algebraically the second time, or at the very least pick different numbers. If you don't know, or are not comfortable with a different method, then use the same method, but do the problem from the beginning and do not look at your original solution. If your two answers don't match up, then you know that this a problem you need to spend a little more time on to figure out where your error is.

This may seem time consuming, but that's ok. It is better to spend more time checking over a few problems than to rush through a lot of problems and repeat the same mistakes.

6. Guess when appropriate

Answering a multiple choice question wrong will result in a 1/4 point penalty. This is to discourage random guessing. If you have no idea how to do a problem, no intuition as to what the correct answer might be, and you can't even eliminate a single answer choice, then *DO NOT* just take a guess. Omit the question and move on.

If, however, you can eliminate even one answer choice, you should take a guess from the remaining four. You should of course eliminate as many choices as you can before you take your guess.

You are not penalized for getting a grid-in question wrong. Therefore you should always guess on grid-in questions that you don't know. Never leave any of these blank. If you have an idea of how large of a number the answer should be, then take a reasonable guess. If not, then just guess anything—don't think too hard—just put in a number.

7. Pace yourself

Do not waste your time on a question that is too hard or will take too long. After you've been working on a question for about 1 minute you need to make a decision. If you understand the question and think that you can get the answer in another 30 seconds or so, continue to work on the problem. If you still don't know how to do the problem or you are using a technique that is going to take a long time, mark it off and come back to it later if you have time.

If you have eliminated at least one answer choice, or it is a grid-in, feel free to take a guess. But you still want to leave open the possibility of coming back to it later. Remember that every problem is worth the same amount. Don't sacrifice problems that you may be able to do by getting hung up on a problem that is too hard for you.

8. Attempt the right number of questions

There are three math sections on the SAT. They can appear in any order. There is a 20 question multiple choice section, a 16 question multiple choice section, and an 18 question section that has 8 multiple choice questions and 10 grid-ins.

Let us call these sections A, B, and C, respectively. You should first make sure that you know what you got on your last SAT practice test, actual SAT, or actual PSAT (whichever you took last). What follows is a general goal you should go for when taking the exam.

Score	Section A	Section B	Section C (Multiple choice)	Section C (Grid-in)
< 330	7/20	6/16	2/8	2/10
330 – 370	10/20	8/16	3/8	3/10
380 – 430	12/20	10/16	4/8	4/10
440 – 490	14/20	11/16	5/8	6/10
500 – 550	16/20	12/16	6/8	8/10
560 – 620	18/20	15/16	7/8	9/10
630 – 800	20/20	16/16	8/8	10/10

For example, a student with a current score of 450 should attempt the first 14 questions from section A, the first 11 questions from section B, the first 5 multiple choice questions from section C, and the first 6 grid-ins from section C.

This is *just* a general guideline. Of course it can be fine-tuned. As a simple example, if you are particularly strong at number theory problems, but very weak at geometry problems, then you may want to try every number theory problem no matter where it appears, and you may want to reduce the number of geometry problems you attempt.

9.   Use your calculator wisely.

It is recommended that you use a TI-84 or comparable calculator for the SAT. It is important that you are comfortable with your calculator on test day, so make sure that you are consistently practicing with the calculator you plan to use. Make sure that your calculator has fresh batteries the day of the test. Nobody will supply a calculator for you if yours dies. Below are the most important things you should practice on your graphing calculator.

(1) Practice entering complicated computations in a single step, and know when to insert parentheses. In general, there are 4 instances when you should use parentheses in your calculator.

- Around numerators of fractions
- Around denominators of fractions
- Around exponents
- Whenever you actually see parentheses in the expression

Examples:
We will substitute a 5 in for x in each of the following examples.

Expression	Calculator computation
$\dfrac{7x+3}{2x-11}$	(7*5 + 3)/(2*5 – 11)
$(3x-8)^{2x-9}$	(3*5 – 8)^(2*5 – 9)

(2) Clear the screen before using it in a new problem. The big screen allows you to check over your computations easily.
(3) Press the **ANS** button (**2nd (-)**) to use your last answer in the next computation.

13

(4) Press **2nd ENTER** to bring up your last computation for editing. This is especially useful when you are plugging in answer choices, or guessing and checking.

(5) You can press **2nd ENTER** over and over again to cycle backwards through all the computations you have ever done.

(6) Know where the $\sqrt{}$, π , and ^ buttons are so you can reach them quickly.

(7) Change a decimal to a fraction by pressing **MATH ENTER ENTER**.

(8) Press the **MATH** button - in the first menu that appears you can take cube roots and nth roots for any n. Scroll right to **PRB** and you have **nPr** and **nCr** to compute permutations and combinations very quickly.

The following items are less important but can be useful.

(9) Press the **Y=** button to enter a function, and then hit **ZOOM 6** to graph it in a standard window.

(10) Practice using the **WINDOW** button to adjust the viewing window of your graph.

(11) Practice using the **TRACE** button to move along the graph and look at some of the points plotted.

(12) Pressing **2nd TRACE** (which is really **CALC**) will bring up a menu of useful items. For example selecting **ZERO** will tell you where the graph hits the x-axis, or equivalently where the function is zero. Selecting **MINIMUM** or **MAXIMUM** can find the vertex of a parabola. Selecting **INTERSECT** will find the point of intersection of 2 graphs.

10. Grid your answers correctly

The computer only grades what you have marked in the bubbles. The space above the bubbles is just for your convenience, and to help you do your bubbling correctly.

Never mark more than one circle in a column or the problem will automatically be marked wrong. You do not need to use all four columns. If you don't use a column just leave it blank.

The symbols that you can grid in are the digits 0

through 9, a decimal point, and a division symbol for fractions. Note that there is no negative symbol. So answers to grid-ins *cannot* be negative. Also, there are only four slots, so you can't get an answer such as 52,326.

Sometimes there is more than one correct answer to a grid-in question. Simply choose one of them to grid-in. *Never* try to fit more than one answer into the grid.

If your answer is a whole number such as 2451 or a decimal that only requires four or less slots such as 2.36, then simply enter the number starting at any column. The two examples just written must be started in the first column, but the number 16 can be entered starting in column 1, 2 or 3.

Note that there is no zero in column 1, so if your answer is 0 it must be gridded into column 2, 3 or 4.

Fractions can be gridded in any form as long as there are enough slots. The fraction 2/100 must be reduced to 1/50 simply because the first representation won't fit in the grid.

Fractions can also be converted to decimals before being gridded in. If a decimal cannot fit in the grid, then you can simply *truncate* it to fit. But you must use every slot in this case. For example, the decimal .167777777... can be gridded as .167, but .16 or .17 would both be marked wrong.

Instead of truncating decimals you can also *round* them. For example, the decimal above could be gridded as .168. Truncating is preferred because there is no thinking involved and you are less likely to make a careless error.

Here are three ways to grid in the number 8/9.

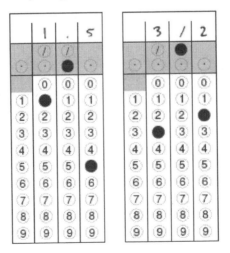

Never grid-in mixed numerals. If your answer is 2 ¼, and you grid in the mixed numeral 2 ¼, then this will be read as 21/4 and will be marked wrong. You must either grid in the decimal 2.25 or the improper fraction 9/4.

Here are two ways to grid in the mixed numeral 1 ½ correctly.

16

PROBLEMS BY LEVEL AND TOPIC WITH FULLY EXPLAINED SOLUTIONS

Note: The quickest solution will always be marked with an asterisk (*).

LEVEL 1: NUMBER THEORY

1. Which of the following numbers is less than 0.216?

   (A) 0.2106
   (B) 0.2161
   (C) 0.2166
   (D) 0.22
   (E) 0.221

We can compare two decimals by looking at the first position where they disagree. For example, 0.215 is less than 0.216 because 5 is less than 6. If a digit is missing, there is a hidden 0 there. Thus 0.2 is also less than 0.216 because 0.2 is the same as 0.200 and 0 is less than 1 (remember that we look at the **first** position where the decimals disagree). Thus the answer here is choice (A) since 0 is less than 6.

* Quick Solution: Answers are given in increasing or decreasing order on the SAT (in this problem they are given in increasing order). Therefore choice (A) is the only reasonable answer.

Remark: The words "less than" would seem to indicate we should start by looking at the smallest answer choice. In this case that is choice (A).

For more information, see **Strategy 2** in **"The 32 Most Effective SAT Math Strategies."**

2. What is the greatest positive integer that is a divisor of 10, 25, and 45?

   (A) 1
   (B) 2
   (C) 3
   (D) 5
   (E) 10

Beginner Method: Pull out your calculator. Since the question has the word **"greatest"** in it, we will start with the greatest answer choice which is choice (E), and we will divide each of the three numbers by 10. Since 25 divided by 10 is 2.5 (not an integer), choice (E) is not the answer. We next try choice (D). The divisions give us 2, 5 and 9 respectively. Since these are all integers, the answer is choice (D).

Note that the three given integers are all divisible by 1, but choice (A) is not the answer because 5 is greater.

Here we have used **Strategy 2** in **"The 32 Most Effective SAT Math Strategies."**

* Intermediate Method: As in the beginner method, we begin with the greatest answer choice. Since 25 (as well as 45) does not end in a 0, it is not divisible by 10. Since all three integers end in a 0 or a 5, they are all divisible by 5. Thus, the answer is choice (D).

Advanced Method: We are being asked to find the **greatest common factor** of 10, 25 and 45, which is 5, choice (D).

Finding the greatest common factor: Here are two ways to find the greatest common factor of the given integers.

   (1) List all factors of each integer and look for the biggest one they have in common.

Factors of 10: {1, 2, 5 10}
Factors of 25: {1, 5, 25}
Factors of 45: {1, 3, 5, 9, 15, 45}

Common Factors: {1, 5}

Thus, the greatest common factor is 5.

(2) Here is a more sophisticated method that is much quicker if the given integers are large.

Step 1: Find the prime factorization of each number in the set.

$$10 = 2*5$$
$$25 = 5^2$$
$$45 = 3^2*5$$

Step 2: Choose the lowest power of each prime that appears in **all** of the factorizations. In this case, this is just 5.

Step 3: Multiply these numbers together to get the greatest common factor. (In this case there is nothing to multiply since there is only one prime factor that the three integers have in common.)

Remark: We can also write the above prime factorizations as follows:

$$10 = 2^1 3^0 5^1$$
$$25 = 2^0 3^0 5^2$$
$$45 = 2^0 3^2 5^1$$

It is easy to see in this form that the lowest power of 2 is $2^0 = 1$, and similarly the lowest power of 3 is 3^0.

3. A positive integer is called a palindrome if it reads the same forward as it does backward. For example, 2442 is a palindrome. Which of the following integers is a palindrome?

    (A) 1010
    (B) 1011
    (C) 2002
    (D) 2020
    (E) 2021

19

* Begin by looking at choice (C). It reads the same forward and backward. Therefore choice (C) is the answer.

Here we have used **Strategy 1** in **"The 32 Most Effective SAT Math Strategies."**

4.   Which of the following numbers is between $\frac{1}{7}$ and $\frac{1}{6}$?

    (A) 0.13
    (B) 0.15
    (C) 0.17
    (D) 0.19
    (E) 0.21

* Change the two fractions to decimals by dividing in your calculator (**decimals are much easier to compare than fractions**). When you divide 1 by 7 you get about 0.1429. When you divide 1 by 6 you get about 0.1667. Since 0.15 is between these two the answer is choice (B).

For more information on this technique, see **Strategy 15** in **"The 32 Most Effective SAT Math Strategies."**

5.   Which of the following numbers disproves the statement "A number that is divisible by 4 and 8 is also divisible by 12"?

    (A) 24
    (B) 48
    (C) 56
    (D) 72
    (E) 96

We want a number that is divisible by 4 and 8, but **not** by 12. Use your calculator and begin with choice (C). When we divide 56 by 4, 8 and 12 we get 14, 7 and about 4.67. Since 14 and 7 are integers we see that 56 is divisible by 4 and 8. Since 4.67 is **not** an integer 56 is not divisible by 12. Thus, choice (C) is the answer.

Here we have used **Strategy 1** in **"The 32 Most Effective SAT Math Strategies."**

20

* Slight upgrade: Any integer which is divisible by 8 is automatically divisible by 4. Thus, we need only check that 56 is divisible by 8 and that 56 is not divisible by 12.

6. $(3+4)^2 =$

* Without a calculator: $(3 + 4)^2 = 7^2 =$ **49**.

Remark: Ideally, you should do the above computation in your head.

With a calculator: Type $(3 + 4)\wedge 2$ into your calculator. The output is **49**.

7. Each of A, B, C, D and E are distinct numbers from the set {2, 15, 25, 31, 34} such that A is prime, B is even, C and D are multiples of 5, and A < E < B. What is E?

* Remember that a prime number is a positive integer with **exactly** 2 factors (1 and itself). Since A is prime, it is either 2 or 31. Since B is even and greater than A it must be 34. Since C and D are multiples of 5 they must be 15 and 25 (not necessarily in that order). So E must be **31**.

Definitions: A **prime number** is a positive integer that has **exactly** two factors (1 and itself). Here is a list of the first few primes:

2, 3, 5, 7, 11, 13, 17, 19, 23,...

Note that 1 is **not** prime. It only has one factor!

A **composite number** has **more** than two factors. Here is a list of the first few composites:

4, 6, 8, 9, 10, 12, 14, 15, 16,...

8. Three consecutive integers are listed in increasing order. If their sum is 732, what is the second integer in the list?

Beginner Method: Let us try some guesses for the second integer.

2nd integer	1st integer	3rd integer	Sum
200	199	201	600
250	249	251	750
240	239	241	720
245	244	246	735
244	243	245	732

Thus, the answer is **244**.

Remark: You should use your calculator to compute these sums. This will be quicker and you are less likely to make a careless error.

Here we have used **Strategy 3** in **"The 32 Most Effective SAT Math Strategies."**

Intermediate Method: If we name the least integer x, then the second and third integers are x + 1 and x + 2, respectively. So we have

$$x + (x + 1) + (x + 2) = 732$$
$$3x + 3 = 732$$
$$3x = 729$$
$$x = 243$$

The second integer is x + 1 = **244**.

* Advanced Method: Simply divide 732 by 3 to get **244**.

Remark for the advanced student: The following algebraic steps show why the advanced method gives the correct solution.

$$x + (x + 1) + (x + 2) = 732$$
$$3x + 3 = 732$$
$$3(x + 1) = 732$$
$$x + 1 = 244.$$

Note that the last two steps show that x + 1 = 732/3.

LEVEL 1: ALGEBRA AND FUNCTIONS

9.   If $3 + x + x + x = 1 + x + x + x + x + x$, what is the value of x ?

    (A) 1
    (B) 2
    (C) 3
    (D) 4
    (E) 5

Beginner Method: Begin by looking at choice (C). We substitute 3 in for x on both sides of the equation.

$$3 + 3 + 3 + 3 = 1 + 3 + 3 + 3 + 3 + 3$$
$$12 = 16$$

Since this is false, we can eliminate choice (C). A little thought should allow you to eliminate choices (D) and (E) as well. We'll try choice (B) next.

$$3 + 2 + 2 + 2 = 1 + 2 + 2 + 2 + 2 + 2$$
$$9 = 11$$

Finally, let us check that choice (A) is correct.

$$3 + 1 + 1 + 1 = 1 + 1 + 1 + 1 + 1 + 1$$
$$6 = 6$$

Thus, the answer is choice (A).

For more information on this technique, see **Strategy 1** in **"The 32 Most Effective SAT Math Strategies."**

Advanced Method: Here is a quick algebraic solution to the problem.

$$3 + x + x + x = 1 + x + x + x + x + x$$
$$3 + 3x = 1 + 5x$$
$$2 = 2x$$
$$1 = x$$

23

Thus, the answer is choice (A).

Remark: We can begin with an algebraic solution, and then switch to the easier method. For example, we can write 3 + 3x = 1 + 5x, and then start substituting in the answer choices from here. This will take less time than the beginner method, but more time than the advanced method.

* **Striking off x's:** When the same term appears on both sides of an equation we can simply delete that term from both sides. In this problem we can strike off 3 x's from each side to get 3 = 1 + x + x. This becomes 2 = 2x from which we see that x = 1, choice (A).

10. If $2t = 8$ and $3s + t = 13$, what is the value of s ?

    (A) 2
    (B) 3
    (C) 4
    (D) 5
    (E) 6

Beginner Method: Looking at the first equation we see that t must be 4 (since 2*4 = 8). Substituting t = 4 into the second equation we get

$$3s + 4 = 13$$

Now let's start with choice (C) as our first guess. We substitute 4 in for s.

$$3*4 + 4 = 13$$
$$12 + 4 = 13$$
$$16 = 13$$

Since 16 is too big we can eliminate choices (C), (D) and (E).

We next try choice (B) and substitute 3 in for s.

$$3*3 + 4 = 13$$
$$9 + 4 = 13$$
$$13 = 13$$

Since we get a true statement, the answer is choice (B).

For more information on this technique, see **Strategy 1** in **"The 32 Most Effective SAT Math Strategies."**

* **Advanced Method:** Solving the first equation for t we get t = 4 (because t = 8/4 = 2). Substituting t = 4 into the second equation we get

$$3s + 4 = 13$$
$$3s = 9$$
$$s = 3$$

Thus, the answer is choice (B).

Remark: The more advanced student should be able to do all of these computations in his/her head.

11. John has fewer nickels than Phil, but more than Thomas. If J, P and T represent the number of nickels that each boy has, respectively, which of the following is true?

    (A) J < T < P
    (B) J < P < T
    (C) P < J < T
    (D) T < P < J
    (E) T < J < P

* When using the symbols "<" and ">", the symbol always points to the smaller number. We will only use the symbol "<" since this is the only symbol that appears in the answer choices. Since John has fewer nickels than Phil we have J < P. Since John has more nickels than Thomas we have T < J. Putting these two together gives us T < J < P. Thus, the answer is choice (E).

Remark: It might seem more natural to write J > T because of the wording in the problem. This is fine, but you then just need to realize that T < J means the same thing. Note again that in the end we want to have only the symbol "<" because this is the only symbol appearing in the answer choices.

12. If $5b - 20 = 15$, then $10 - 2b =$

    (A) -4
    (B) -2
    (C) 0
    (D) 2
    (E) 4

Beginner Method: Unfortunately, in this problem we can't simply use the answer choices as our "guesses" for b. We can, however, still make our own educated guesses. Let us start with a "random" guess for b, for example b = 10. So let's plug 10 in for b in the first equation.

$$5b - 20 = 15$$
$$5*10 - 20 = 15$$
$$50 - 20 = 15$$
$$30 = 15$$

Our guess was too big. So let's take a smaller guess like 5.

$$5b - 20 = 15$$
$$5*5 - 20 = 15$$
$$25 - 20 = 15$$
$$5 = 15$$

Now our guess was too small. It looks like 7 should do the trick.

$$5b - 20 = 15$$
$$5*7 - 20 = 15$$
$$35 - 20 = 15$$
$$15 = 15$$

It worked. So b is 7. Thus 10 − 2b = 10 − 2*7 = 10 − 14 = -4. So the answer is choice (A).

For more information on this technique, see **Strategy 3** in **"The 32 Most Effective SAT Math Strategies."**

* **Advanced Method:** Here is an algebraic solution. We solve the first equation for b.

$$5b - 20 = 15$$
$$5b = 35$$
$$b = 7$$

Then $10 - 2b = 10 - 2*7 = 10 - 14 = -4$. So the answer is choice (A).

13. If $3 + x = 12$, what is the value of $5x$?

(A) 9
(B) 18
(C) 36
(D) 45
(E) 144

* From the first equation we see that x = 9. So 5x = 5*9 = 45, choice (D).

14. If $8^2 = 4^y$, then $y =$

* $8^2 = 64 = 4^3$. So y = **3**.

An algebraic solution: I don't recommend an algebraic solution in this case, but let's include it for completeness.

We rewrite each side of the equation with base 2.

$$8^2 = (2^3)^2 = 2^6 \text{ and } 4^y = (2^2)^y = 2^{2y}.$$

So 2y = 6, and therefore y = **3**.

15. If $x + 6 = 17$, then $(x + 2)^2 =$

Beginner Method: From the given equation we see that x = 11. Then

$$(x + 2)^2 = (11 + 2)^2 = 13^2 = \textbf{169}.$$

* **Advanced Method:** We solve the given equation for x + 2 by subtracting 4 from each side. Thus x + 2 = 13. Therefore

$$(x + 2)^2 = 13^2 = \mathbf{169}.$$

16. If $\dfrac{s}{t} = \dfrac{5}{19}$ and $\dfrac{t}{u} = \dfrac{19}{40}$, then $\dfrac{s}{u} =$

Solution by multiplication:

s/u = (s/t)*(t/u) = (5/19)*(19/40) = 5/40 = **1/8** (or **.125**).

* **Solution by picking numbers:** The choices s = 5, t = 19, and u = 40 are consistent with the given information. Then s/u = 5/40 = **1/8**.

For more information on this technique, see **Strategy 4** in **"The 32 Most Effective SAT Math Strategies."**

LEVEL 1: GEOMETRY

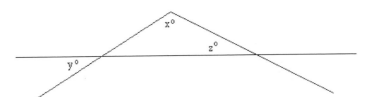

Note: Figure not drawn to scale.

17. In the figure above, if $y = 30$ and $z = 45$, what is the value of x ?

    (A) 15
    (B) 30
    (C) 60
    (D) 105
    (E) 125

* We begin by substituting in 30 degrees for y and 45 degrees for z in the given figure. The non-labeled angle in the triangle is also 30 degrees because it forms a pair of **vertical angles** with the angle labeled by y.

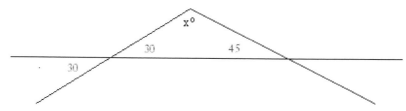

Note: Figure not drawn to scale.

The angles of a triangle add up to 180 degrees. Thus

x = 180 – 30 – 45 = 105, choice (D).

18. If the degree measures of the three angles of a triangle are $50°$, $z°$, and $z°$, what is the value of z ?

(A) 60
(B) 65
(C) 70
(D) 75
(E) 80

Beginner Method: Recall that a triangle has 180 degrees. Let us start with choice (C). If we take a guess that z = 70, then the sum of the angles is equal to 50 + z + z = 50 + 70 + 70 = 190 degrees, a bit too large. We can therefore eliminate choices (C), (D), and (E). Let us try choice (B) next. So we are guessing that z = 65. It follows that the sum of the angles is equal to 50 + z + z = 50 + 65 + 65 = 180 degrees. Since this is correct, the answer is choice (B).

For more information on this technique, see **Strategy 1** in **"The 32 Most Effective SAT Math Strategies."**

* Advanced Method: There are 180 degrees in a triangle, so we solve the following equation.

$$50 + z + z = 180$$
$$50 + 2z = 180$$
$$2z = 130$$
$$z = 65$$

Therefore the answer is choice (B).

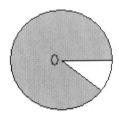

19. O is the center of the circle above. Approximately what percent of the circle is shaded?

   (A) 10%
   (B) 25%
   (C) 50%
   (D) 75%
   (E) 90%

* We can assume that the figure is drawn to scale. The answer is certainly more than 75%. Thus the answer must be choice (E).

For more information on this technique, see **Strategy 6** in **"The 32 Most Effective SAT Math Strategies."**

Clarification: If you are having trouble seeing that the answer is more than 75% just look at the following figure.

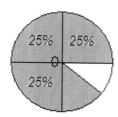

20. The volume of a rectangular box is 2 cubic inches. If the width of the box is 4 inches and the height is $\frac{1}{4}$ inch, what is the length?

(A) $\frac{1}{8}$ inch

(B) $\frac{1}{4}$ inch

(C) 1 inch

(D) 2 inches

(E) 4 inches

* The formula for the volume of a box is given at the beginning of each math section on the SAT.

$$V = \ell wh$$
$$2 = \ell\,(4)(1/4)$$
$$2 = \ell$$

Therefore the answer is choice (D).

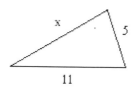

21. If the perimeter of the triangle on the left is twice the perimeter of the triangle on the right, what is the value of x ?

* Recall that you compute the **perimeter** of a triangle by adding up the lengths of its three sides. The perimeter of the triangle on the right is

$$6 + 6 + 3 = 15.$$

Thus the perimeter of the triangle on the left is 2*15 = 30. So

$$x = 30 - 11 - 5 = \textbf{14}.$$

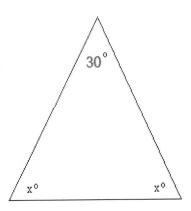

22.   In the triangle above, what is the value of x ?

Beginner Method: Recall that a triangle has 180 degrees. We take a guess for x, let's say x = 60. It then follows that the sum of the angles is x + x + 30 = 60 + 60 + 30 = 150 degrees, a bit too small. Let's try x = 80. Then the sum of the angles is x + x + 30 = 80 + 80 + 30 = 190 degree, too big. Let's try x = 75. Then the sum is x + x + 30 = 75 + 75 + 30 = 180. Thus, the answer is **75**.

For more information on this technique, see **Strategy 3** in **"The 32 Most Effective SAT Math Strategies."**

* **Advanced Method:** There are 180 degrees in a triangle, so we solve the following equation.

$$x + x + 30 = 180$$
$$2x + 30 = 180$$
$$2x = 150$$
$$x = \textbf{75}.$$

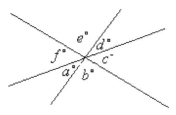

Note: Figure not drawn to scale.

23. In the figure above, three lines intersect at a point. If $a = 35$ and $c = 55$, what is the value of e ?

* Since **vertical angles** have the same degree measure, we see that

f = c = 55.

Since straight lines have 180 degrees, a, f and e must add to 180. So

e = 180 − a − f = 180 − 35 − 55 = **90**.

Alternatives:

(1) We can use vertical angles to see that d = a = 35. Then

e = 180 − d − c = **90**.

(2) We can use vertical angles to see that f = c = 55, d = a = 35, and e = b. So

b + e = 360 − a − c − d − f = 360 − 35 − 55 − 35 − 55 = 180
  2e = 180
   e = **90**.

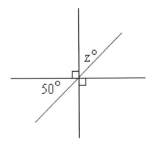

24. In the figure above, what is the value of *z* ?

* Since vertical angles are congruent, we get the following picture.

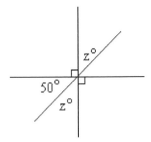

So z + 50 = 90, and z = **40**.

LEVEL 1: PROBABILITY AND STATISTICS

25. The average (arithmetic mean) of three numbers is 100. If two of the numbers are 80 and 130, what is the third number?

(A) 70
(B) 80
(C) 90
(D) 100
(E) 110

* We change the average to a sum using the formula

$$\text{Sum} = \text{Average} * \text{Number}$$

We are averaging 3 numbers so that the Number is 3. The Average is given to be 100. Therefore the Sum of the 3 numbers is 100*3 = 300. Since we know that two of the numbers are 80 and 130, the third number is 300 − 80 − 130 = 90, choice (C).

Note: The above formula comes from eliminating the denominator in the definition of average.

$$\text{Average} = \text{Sum/Number}$$

For more information on this technique, see **Strategy 20** in **"The 32 Most Effective SAT Math Strategies."**

26. A menu lists 6 meals and 5 drinks. How many different meal-drink combinations are possible from this menu?

    (A) 30
    (B) 15
    (C) 11
    (D) 6
    (E) 5

* We will use the **counting principle** which says that if one event is followed by a second independent event, the number of possibilities is multiplied. So in this example, the answer is 6*5=30, choice (A).

Remark: The 2 events here are "choosing a meal," and "choosing a drink."

Creating a list: If you are having trouble understanding why we multiply in this problem, try writing out your own list and it should become clear. So, for example, suppose that our six meal choices are chicken, beef, fish, pasta, salad, and soup. Suppose our five drink choices are water, juice, soda, coffee, and tea. Here is a beginning of the list of meal-drink combinations. See if you can finish this list:

Chicken and water
Chicken and juice
Chicken and soda
Chicken and coffee
Chicken and tea
Beef and water
Beef and juice..........

For more information on this technique, see **Strategy 21** in **"The 32 Most Effective SAT Math Strategies."**

27. Stickers in the shape of an isosceles triangle, a hexagon, a parallelogram, and a trapezoid are placed into a bucket. If one of these stickers is taken out at random, what is the probability that the shape chosen will have less than 4 vertices?

    (A) $\dfrac{3}{13}$

    (B) $\dfrac{1}{4}$

    (C) $\dfrac{5}{11}$

    (D) $\dfrac{1}{2}$

    (E) $\dfrac{3}{4}$

* There are 4 stickers in total and only one of them has a shape with less than 4 vertices. Thus, the answer is 1/4, choice (B).

Notes:

(1) A triangle has 3 vertices, a quadrilateral has 4 vertices, and a hexagon has 6 vertices.

(2) An isosceles triangle is a triangle with 2 congruent sides (or equivalently, 2 congruent angles). The triangle being isosceles is **not** important for this problem. All that is important is that it has 3 vertices.

(3) A parallelogram is a quadrilateral with 2 pairs of congruent sides (or equivalently 2 pairs of parallel sides). All that is needed for this problem is that a parallelogram has 4 vertices.

(4) A trapezoid is a quadrilateral with 1 pair of parallel sides and 1 pair of nonparallel sides. All that is needed for this problem is that a trapezoid has 4 vertices.

$$3, 4, 5, 6, 7, 8, 9, 10, 11$$

28. If a number is selected at random from the list above, what is the probability that it will be greater than 8?

(A) $\frac{2}{9}$

(B) $\frac{1}{3}$

(C) $\frac{4}{9}$

(D) $\frac{2}{3}$

(E) 1

* There are 9 numbers in total and 3 of them are greater than 8 (the numbers greater than 8 are 9, 10, and 11). Thus, the answer is 3/9 which reduces to 1/3, choice (B).

Notes:

(1) You can reduce the fraction in your graphing calculator by dividing 3 by 9, then pressing the Math button, followed by the Enter button twice.

$$3 \div 9 \quad \text{Enter} \quad \text{Math} \quad \text{Enter} \quad \text{Enter}$$

(2) To compute a simple probability where all outcomes are equally likely, divide the number of "successes" by the total number of outcomes. In this case there are 3 "successes," namely 9, 10, and 11. There are a total of 9 outcomes.

29. For which of the following lists of 5 numbers is the average (arithmetic mean) less than the median?

(A) 1, 1, 3, 4, 4
(B) 1, 2, 3, 5, 6
(C) 1, 1, 3, 5, 5
(D) 1, 2, 3, 4, 5
(E) 1, 2, 3, 4, 9

All of these lists have a median of 3 (this is the number in the middle when the numbers are written in increasing order).

It is very often easiest to work with the **Sum** of the numbers instead of the Average. We can easily change an average to a sum using the following simple formula.

Sum = Average * Number

In this case we want the sum to be less than 3*5 = 15.

Let's start with choice (C). The sum is 1 + 1 + 3 + 5 + 5 = 15.
Let's try (D) next. 1 + 2 + 3 + 4 + 5 = 15
Let's try (B). 1 + 2 + 3 + 5 + 6 = 17
Let's try (A). 1 + 1 + 3 + 4 + 4 = 13.

Since 13 is less than 15, the answer is choice (A).

For more information on this technique, see **Strategies 1 and 20** in "The 32 Most Effective SAT Math Strategies."

* Quick Solution: With a little experience it is not hard to see that (A) is the answer. Just look at how the numbers are "balanced" about the middle number 3. 1 is two units to the left, and 4 is only 1 unit to the right. You should still compute the sum as a check to verify that the answer is correct.

30. The average (arithmetic mean) of seven numbers is 200. If the sum of six of the numbers is 1292, what is the seventh number?

* We change the average to a sum using the formula

Sum = Average * Number

Here we are averaging 7 numbers. Thus the Number is 7. The Average is given to be 200. Therefore the Sum of the 7 numbers is 200*7 = 1400. Since we know that the sum of six of the numbers is 1292, the seventh number is

$$1400 - 1292 = \mathbf{108}.$$

Note: The above formula comes from eliminating the denominator in the definition of average.

Average = Sum/Number

For more information on this technique, see **Strategy 20** in **"The 32 Most Effective SAT Math Strategies."**

31. In a jar there are exactly 54 marbles, each of which is either orange, purple, or white. The probability of randomly selecting an orange marble from the jar is $\frac{1}{9}$, and the probability of randomly selecting a purple marble from the jar is $\frac{2}{9}$. How many marbles in the jar are white?

There are 54(1/9) = 6 orange marbles in the jar, and 54(2/9) = 12 purple marbles in the jar. Therefore, the number of white marbles in the jar is $54 - 6 - 12 = \mathbf{36}$.

* Another method: The probability of selecting a white marble from the jar is 1 − 1/9 − 2/9 = 1 − 3/9 = 2/3 (do this computation on your calculator). Thus, there are 54(2/3) = **36** white marbles in the jar.

32. Joe, Mike, Phil, and John own a total of 137 CDs. If John owns 38 of them, what is the average (arithmetic mean) number of CDs owned by Joe, Mike, and Phil?

* 137 − 38 = 99 is the total number of CDs owned by Joe, Mike, and Phil. We can compute the average using the formula

Average = Sum/Number

Here the Sum is 99 and the Number is 3. So the average is 99/3 = **33**.

LEVEL 2: NUMBER THEORY

$$\frac{6}{n}, \quad \frac{7}{n}, \quad \frac{11}{n}$$

33. If each of the fractions above is in its simplest reduced form, then which of the following could be the value of n ?

   (A) 15
   (B) 25
   (C) 27
   (D) 35
   (E) 55

Beginner Method: A fraction is in simplest reduced form if the numerator (top) and denominator (bottom) have no common factors greater than 1. For example 6/27 is not reduced since 6 and 27 are both divisible by 3. This eliminates choice (C). Since 7 and 35 are both divisible by 7 we can eliminate choice (D) as well. Since 25 has no factors in common with 6, 7 or 11 we see that choice (B) is the answer.

For more information on this technique, see **Strategy 1** in **"The 32 Most Effective SAT Math Strategies."**

* Advanced Method: 6, 7 and 11 have prime factors of 2, 3, 7 and 11. So we simply pick the answer choice whose prime factorization does not consist of any of these integers. Since the only prime factor of 25 is 5, choice (B) is the answer.

34. If k is an odd integer, what is the greatest odd integer less than k ?

    (A) $k-3$
    (B) $k-2$
    (C) $k-1$
    (D) $2(k-1)$
    (E) $2(k-1)-3$

Beginner Method: We will use the technique of **picking numbers**. Let's set k equal to 5 (note that we must choose an odd integer for k). The greatest odd integer less than 5 is 3. So we will eliminate any answer choice that is not 3. The answer choices turn into the following:

    (A) 2
    (B) 3
    (C) 4
    (D) 2(4) = 8
    (E) 2(4) − 3 = 8 − 3 = 5

Since (B) is the only choice that has become 3, we conclude that choice (B) is the answer.

Important note: (B) is **not** the correct answer simply because it is equal to 3. It is correct because all 4 of the other choices are **not** 3.

For more information on this technique, see **Strategy 4** in **"The 32 Most Effective SAT Math Strategies."**

* Advanced Method: If k is odd, then 1 less than k is even, and 2 less than k is odd. So k − 2 is the greatest odd integer less than k. Thus, the answer is choice (B).

35. A room has 1200 square feet of surface that needs to be painted. If 2 gallons of paint will cover 450 square feet, what is the least whole number of gallons that must be purchased in order to have enough paint to cover the entire surface?

    (A) 2
    (B) 3
    (C) 4
    (D) 5
    (E) 6

* This is a simple ratio. We begin by identifying 2 key words. In this case, such a pair of key words is "square feet" and "gallons."

| square feet | 1200 | 450 |
| gallons | x | 2 |

Now simply cross multiply and divide the corresponding ratio to find the unknown quantity x.

$$1200/x = 450/2$$
$$2400 = 450x$$
$$x \sim 5.333 \text{ (where the symbol} \sim \text{means "is approximately")}$$

So we will need 6 gallons to cover the entire surface (note that if we round the answer to the nearest integer we get the **incorrect** number 5 – rounding is not correct here because we need **more** than 5 gallons of paint to cover the surface). Thus the answer is choice (E).

For more information on this technique, see **Strategy 14** in **"The 32 Most Effective SAT Math Strategies."**

36. A piece of cable x feet in length is cut into exactly 4 pieces, each 3 feet 5 inches in length. What is the value of x ?

(A) $12\frac{2}{3}$

(B) 13

(C) $13\frac{1}{3}$

(D) $13\frac{2}{3}$

(E) 14

* Since there are 12 inches in a foot, each piece is 3*12 + 5 = 36 + 5 = 41 inches. The total length of the original cable is then 41 * 4 = 164 inches. To convert back to feet we divide 164 by 12 to get approximately 13.67 feet. This is answer choice (D).

Remark: If you don't recognize the decimal portion as 2/3, you can do one of the following:

(a) Divide both 1 and 2 by 3 in your calculator to convert 1/3 and 2/3 to decimals (we choose these because they appear in the answer choices).
(b) On your graphing calculator first subtract 13 to get rid of the integer part of the answer and then convert the decimal to a fraction and you will get 2/3.

37. If x is 40% of z and y is 55% of z , what is $x + y$ in terms of z ?

(A) $.22z$
(B) $.44z$
(C) $.75z$
(D) $.85z$
(E) $.95z$

Let's substitute the number 100 in for z (the number 100 is often a good choice in percent problems – after all, the word percent means "out of 100"). Then y is 55% of 100 which is 55, and x is 40% of 100 which is 40.

Thus x + y = 40 + 55 = **95**. The answer is clearly choice (E), but for the sake of completion let's plug z = 100 into each answer choice.

(A) 22
(B) 44
(C) 75
(D) 85
(E) 95

We see that the answer is choice (E).

For more information on this technique, see **Strategy 4** in **"The 32 Most Effective SAT Math Strategies."**

* **An algebraic solution:** x = .40z and y = .55z. So we have that x + y = .40z + .55z = .95z. Therefore the answer is choice (E).

38. From 8 a.m. to 1 p.m. on Friday, a group of photographers will be taking individual pictures of 900 students. If it takes 5 minutes to take each student's picture, how many photographers are needed?

* There are 5 hours between 8 a.m. and 1 p.m. So there are 5 * 60 = 300 minutes. A single photographer can take 300/5 = 60 pictures in this time. 900/60 = 15. So 15 photographers are needed. Thus, the answer is **15**.

39. A 4-pound mixture requires $2\frac{1}{2}$ liters of water. At this rate, how many liters of water should be used for a 7-pound mixture?

* This is a simple ratio. We begin by identifying 2 key words. In this case, such a pair of key words is "mixture" and "water."

mixture	4	7
water	2.5	x

We now find x by cross multiplying and dividing.

$$4/2.5 = 7/x$$
$$4x = 17.5$$
$$x = 4.375.$$

So we can grid in **4.37** or **4.38**.

For more information on this technique, see **Strategy 14** in **"The 32 Most Effective SAT Math Strategies."**

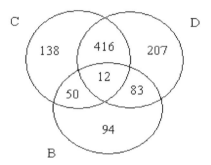

40. 1000 students were polled to determine which of the following animals they had as pets: cats (C), dogs (D), or birds (B). The Venn diagram above shows the results of the poll. How many students said they have exactly 2 of the 3 types of animals?

* 416 of the students have cats and dogs only.
50 of the students have cats and birds only.
83 of the students have dogs and birds only.

$$416 + 50 + 83 = \textbf{549}.$$

LEVEL 2: ALGEBRA AND FUNCTIONS

41. If 8 less than y is 3 more than 9, what is the value of y ?

(A) -19
(B) -4
(C) 20
(D) 24
(E) 35

* Beginner Method: 3 more than 9 is 9 + 3 = 12. So 8 less than y is 12. Well 8 less than 20 is 12. So x = 20, choice (C).

Advanced Method: "a more than b" means b + a. "a less than b" means b – a. The word "is" means =. So we have

$$y - 8 = 9 + 3$$
$$y - 8 = 12$$
$$y = 20$$

Thus, the answer is choice (C).

Remark: 9 + 3 = 3 + 9, so technically 3 more than 9 can also be written as 3 + 9 since it gives the same answer. You have to be more careful with "less than" because y – 8 is not the same as 8 – y. So just remember in the expression "a less than b," the numbers reverse positions when we write the algebraic equivalent.

You should also get in the habit of reversing the positions in "a more than b" the same way. In this way you will probably not make a mistake when a problem with the words "less than" comes up.

42. If $(3a - b)(a - 2b) = c$, which of the following is always equal to $(12a - 4b)(a - 2b)$?

   (A) $2c$
   (B) $3c$
   (C) $4c$
   (D) $8c$
   (E) $12c$

Beginner Method: We will use the technique of **picking numbers**. Let's try a = 4 and b = 5. So (3a − b)(a − 2b) = (3*4 − 5)(4 − 2*5) = (7)(-6) = -42. Therefore c = -42. Also,

$$(12a - 4b)(a - 2b) = (12*4 - 4*5)(4 - 2*5) = (28)(-6) = \textbf{-168}.$$

Put a nice big, dark circle around this number. We now substitute c = -42 into the answer choices.

   (A) -84
   (B) -126
   (C) -168
   (D) -336
   (E) -504

Since (A), (B), (D) and (E) are incorrect we can eliminate them. Therefore the answer is choice (C).

Important note: (C) is **not** the correct answer simply because it is equal to -168. It is correct because all 4 of the other choices are **not** -168.

For more information on this technique, see **Strategy 4** in **"The 32 Most Effective SAT Math Strategies."**

* Advanced Method: (12a − 4b)(a − 2b) = 4(3a − b)(a − 2b) = 4c. This is answer choice (C).

43. If $b > 3$, which of the following represents four times the positive difference between 17 and $7b$?

    (A) $4(17) - 7b$

    (B) $4(7b - 17)$

    (C) $4(7b) - 17$

    (D) $4(10b)$

    (E) $7b - 4(17)$

Beginner Method: We will use the technique of **picking numbers**. Let's try b = 5. Then 7b = 7(5) = 35. The difference between 17 and 7b is

$$7b - 17 = 35 - 17 = 18.$$

Four times the difference between 17 and 7b is then 4*18 = **72**. Put a nice big, dark circle around this number. We now substitute b = 5 into each answer choice.

    (A) 33

    (B) 72

    (C) 123

    (D) 200

    (E) -33

Since (A), (C), (D) and (E) are incorrect we can eliminate them. Therefore the answer is choice (B).

Important note: (B) is **not** the correct answer simply because it is equal to 44. It is correct because all 4 of the other choices are **not** 44.

For more information on this technique, see **Strategy 4** in **"The 32 Most Effective SAT Math Strategies."**

* Advanced Method: The difference between 17 and 7b is either $17 - 7b$ or $7b - 17$. Since b > 3, 7b > 17, and therefore the **positive** difference is $7b - 17$. Four times this positive difference is then $4(7b - 17)$, choice (B).

44. If $x \neq 0$, which of the following is equivalent to $5x$?

    (A) x^5

    (B) $\dfrac{x}{5}$

    (C) $x+5$

    (D) $\dfrac{x+x+x}{x+x}$

    (E) $x+x+x+x+x$

Beginner Method: We will use the technique of **picking numbers**. Let's try x = 2. Then 5x = 5(2) = **10**. Put a nice big, dark circle around this number. We now substitute x = 2 into each answer choice.

    (A) 32
    (B) .4
    (C) 7
    (D) 1.5
    (E) 10

Since (A), (B), (C) and (D) are incorrect we can eliminate them. Therefore the answer is choice (E).

Important note: (E) is **not** the correct answer simply because it is equal to 10. It is correct because all 4 of the other choices are **not** 10.

For more information on this technique, see **Strategy 4** in **"The 32 Most Effective SAT Math Strategies."**

* **Advanced Method:** Multiplying x by 5 is the same as adding x to itself 5 times. This is choice (E).

45. Billy has 130 candies that he wants to distribute among Bobby, Johnny and Freddie. He wants to give Freddie three times as much as he gives Johnny and one third as much as he gives Bobby. How much should he give Freddie?

    (A) 9
    (B) 15
    (C) 21
    (D) 27
    (E) 30

* Let's start with choice (C) as our first guess. If Freddie has 21 candies, then Johnny has 7 candies and Bobby has 63 candies. This gives a total of 21 + 7 + 63 = 91 candies. This is too small so we can eliminate choices (A), (B), and (C). Since 91 is quite a bit smaller than 130, let's try choice (E) next. If Freddie has 30 candies, then Johnny has 10 candies and Bobby has 90 candies. This gives a total of 30 + 10 + 90 = 130 candies. This is correct. Therefore the answer is choice (E).

For more information on this technique, see **Strategy 1** in **"The 32 Most Effective SAT Math Strategies."**

An algebraic solution for the advanced student: I do not recommend solving this problem algebraically on the actual SAT, but it is good for the more advanced students to practice solving problems this way to increase their mathematical maturity. Let x, y and z represent the number of candies given to Bobby, Johnny, and Freddy, respectively. Then $z = 3y$ and $z = x/3$. So $y = z/3$ and $x = 3z$. Since there are a total of 130 candies we have that $x + y + z = 130$. Substituting we have

$$3z + z/3 + z = 130.$$

Multiply through by 3 to get rid of the denominator.

$$9z + z + 3z = 390$$
$$13z = 390$$
$$z = 30$$

Since z represents the number of candies that Billy should give Freddie, the answer is 30, choice (E).

Important Note: Before answering the question always make sure that you found the right quantity. If the question had asked "How much should he give to Johnny?," then 30 would be incorrect. In this case we would want y = z/3 = 30/3 = 10.

46. If $\dfrac{2y}{z} = -5$, then $2y + 5z =$

Beginner Method: We will use the technique of **picking numbers**. Let's try y = 10 and z = -4. First note that 2y/z = 20/(-4) = -5. Therefore our choices for y and z are acceptable. Now,

2y + 5z = 2*10 + 5(-4) = 20 – 20 = **0**.

For more information on this technique, see **Strategy 4** in **"The 32 Most Effective SAT Math Strategies."**

* Advanced Method: Multiplying both sides of the equation by z gives us 2y = -5z. We now add 5z to both sides to get 2y + 5z = **0**.

47. At a pet store, each lizard is priced at $1 and each snake is priced at $8. Luis purchased 14 reptiles at the store for a total price of $42. How many lizards did Luis purchase?

* Let's take a guess. Although we can guess the number of lizards, we will probably get the answer quicker if we instead guess the number of snakes (because they're more expensive). Let's guess that Luis purchased 3 snakes. Then he also purchased 11 lizards. The total price would then be 11*1 + 3*8 = 35. This is too little money, so he must have purchased **more** snakes. If Luis purchased 4 snakes, then he purchased 10 lizards, and the total price would be 10*1 + 4*8 = 42, perfect!. So Luis purchased **10** lizards.

For more information on this technique, see **Strategy 3** in **"The 32 Most Effective SAT Math Strategies."**

An algebraic solution: Let x be the number of lizards purchased, and y the number of snakes purchased. Since there are 14 reptiles in total, we must have x + y = 14. We also have x + 8y = 42 because the total price is $42. So we have the following system of equations.

$$x + 8y = 42$$
$$x + y = 14$$

We will use the **elimination method**. Note that we want to find x. In this case however it is quicker to eliminate x and find y. We can do this quickly by subtracting the bottom equation from the top one.

$$x + 8y = 42$$
$$\underline{x + y = 14}$$
$$7y = 28$$

So y = 4. Substituting back into the second equation, we see that x = **10**.

48. If $5(3y + 7) = 15(y + 4k)$, what is the value of $60k$?

* Distributing on the left and right hand sides of the given equation gives us

$$15y + 35 = 15y + 60k.$$

Therefore 60k = **35**.

LEVEL 2: GEOMETRY

49. In an xy coordinate system, which point lies in the interior of a circle with center (0, 0) and radius 3?

(A) (1, -3)
(B) (-1, -2)
(C) (-3, 1)
(D) (0, 3)
(E) (3, 3)

* If one of the coordinates of the point is 3 or -3, then the point is either on or outside of the circle (if the other coordinate is 0 the point is on the circle, otherwise it is outside). We can therefore eliminate choices (A), (C), (D) and (E). Thus, the answer is choice (B).

Remark: A picture can help clarify the above solution if you are confused. Draw the given circle inscribed in a square. The points with a coordinate of 3 or -3 lie on this square.

For the advanced student: In order for a point (x, y) to lie in the interior of a circle with center (0, 0) and radius 3, the distance between (x, y) and (0, 0) needs to be less than 3. We can use the distance formula to check this:

$$d^2 = (x - 0)^2 + (y - 0)^2 = x^2 + y^2$$

We want d to be less than 3, or equivalently d^2 to be less than 9.

Starting with choice (C), we have $d^2 = (-3)^2 + 1^2 = 10$. This is too big.

Let's try choice (B). $d^2 = (-1)^2 + (-2)^2 = 5$. Since this is less than 9, choice (B) is the answer.

A common error: Many students get confused when squaring a negative number. Remember that squaring means "multiplying by itself." So for example, $(-3)^2 = (-3)(-3) = 9$. Compare this to the following computation: $-3^2 = (-1)(3^2) = (-1)(9) = -9$ (negating a number means to multiply by negative 1). Notice that in this last computation we were careful to follow the usual order of operations. We performed the exponentiation before multiplying by -1.

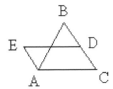

50. In the figure above, $\triangle ABC$ is equilateral and $AEDC$ is a parallelogram. If D is the midpoint of BC and the perimeter of $\triangle ABC$ is 12, what is the perimeter of $AEDC$?

(A) 3
(B) 6
(C) 10
(D) 12
(E) 24

* Each side of triangle ABC has length 12/3 = 4. In particular AC and BC have length 4. Since AC has length 4 and AEDC is a parallelogram, ED also has length 4. Since BC has length 4, and D is the midpoint of BC, DC has length 2. Since AEDC is a parallelogram, AE has length 2. So, the perimeter of AEDC is 2 + 4 + 2 + 4 = 12, choice (D).

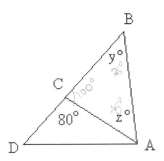

51. In $\triangle ABD$ above, if $y = 35$, what is the value of z ?

(A) 25
(B) 30
(C) 35
(D) 40
(E) 45

54

Beginner Method: Angles ACD and ACB form a linear pair and are therefore supplementary. So angle ACB has measure 180 − 80 = 100 degrees. Since the angles of a triangle add up to 180 degrees, it follows that

$$z = 180 - 35 - 100 = 45.$$

This is answer choice (E).

* Advanced Method: The measure of an exterior angle of a triangle is the sum of the measures of the two opposite interior angles of the triangle. So 80 = 35 + z, and therefore z = 80 − 35 = 45, choice (E).

For more information on this technique, see **Strategy 30** in **"The 32 Most Effective SAT Math Strategies."**

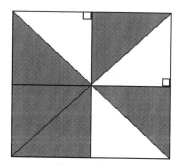

52. What percent of the square above is shaded?

   (A) 25%

   (B) $33 \frac{1}{3}$ %

   (C) 50%

   (D) $62 \frac{1}{2}$ %

   (E) $66 \frac{2}{3}$ %

* 5 of the 8 pieces are shaded and each of these pieces has equal area.

55

5/8 = .625 = 62.5%, choice (D).

Notes:

(1) To change 5/8 to the decimal .625 simply divide 5 by 8 in your calculator.

(2) To change the decimal to a percent move the decimal point two places to the right.

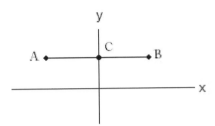

53. In the figure above, if AB is a line segment parallel to the x-axis such that $AC = CB$, and the coordinates of point B are (x, y), then what are the coordinates of point A?

   (A) $(-x, y)$
   (B) $(x, -y)$
   (C) $(-x, -y)$
   (D) (y, x)
   (E) $(y, -x)$

Beginner Method: Let's pick a point. B looks like it could be (4, 2). So to plot B we move right 4 and up 2. Thus, to plot A we move left 4 and up 2, so that A is the point **(-4, 2)**. Put a nice big, dark circle around this point. Now we plug x = 4 and y = 2 into each answer choice, and eliminate any that do not come out to (-4, 2).

   (A) (-4, 2)
   (B) (4, -2)
   (C) (-4, -2)
   (D) (2, 4)
   (E) (2, -4)

So we can eliminate choices (B), (C), (D), and (E). Thus the answer is choice (A).

Important note: (A) is **not** the correct answer simply because it is equal to (-4, 2). It is correct because all 4 of the other choices are **not** (-4, 2).

For more information on this technique, see **Strategy 4** in **"The 32 Most Effective SAT Math Strategies."**

* **Advanced Method:** To plot point B, from the origin we move right x and up y. So, to plot point A, from the origin we move left x and up y. Thus the coordinates of point A are (-x, y), choice (A).

54. The line in the xy-plane that contains the point $(-3, 7)$ and $(5, y)$ has slope 0. What is the value of y?

* All points on a line with slope 0 have the same y-coordinate. So y = **7**.

Remark: A line with slope 0 is a horizontal line.

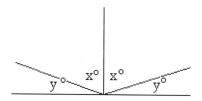

Note: Figure not drawn to scale.

55. In the figure above, $x = 56$. What is the value of y?

* Since a straight line has 180 degrees, we have 2x + 2y = 180. Since we are given that x = 56, we have 2*56 + 2y = 180, or 112 + 2y = 180. Thus, 2y = 68, and y = **34**.

56. In a circle with diameter 30, if r represents the radius of the circle, what is the value of $\frac{7}{5}r$?

* The radius of a circle is half the diameter, so that r = 15. Then

$7/5 * r = 7/5 * 15 = \mathbf{21}$.

LEVEL 2: PROBABILITY AND STATISTICS

57. The average (arithmetic mean) of three numbers is 57. If one of the numbers is 16, what is the sum of the other two?

   (A) 41
   (B) 72
   (C) 107
   (D) 153
   (E) 155

* We change the average to a sum using the formula

Sum = Average * Number

We are averaging 3 numbers so that the Number is 3. The Average is given to be 57. Therefore the Sum of the 3 numbers is 57*3 = 171. Since one of the numbers is 16, the sum of the other two is 171 − 16 = 155, choice (E).

Note: The above formula comes from eliminating the denominator in the definition of average.

Average = Sum/Number

For more information on this technique, see **Strategy 20** in **"The 32 Most Effective SAT Math Strategies."**

A complete algebraic solution for the advanced student: This method is **not** recommended for the SAT, but it is included for completeness. Let x, y, and 16 be the three numbers. Then (x + y + 16)/3 = 57. Multiplying both sides of this equation by 3 yields x + y + 16 = 171. Finally, we subtract 16 from both sides to get x + y = 155, choice (E).

58. What is the average (arithmetic mean) of $9 - k$, 9, and $9 + k$?

    (A) 3
    (B) 9
    (C) 15
    (D) $3 + \dfrac{k}{3}$
    (E) $9 + \dfrac{k}{3}$

Beginner Method: Let's pick a number for k, say k = 6. Then the question is asking for the average of 3, 9, and 15. We get (3 + 9 + 15)/3 = 27/3 = **9**. Put a nice big, dark circle around this number so you can find it easily later. We now substitute k = 6 into each answer choice.

    (A) 3
    (B) 9
    (C) 15
    (D) 3 + 2 = 5
    (E) 9 + 2 = 11

We now compare each of these numbers to the number that we put a nice big, dark circle around. Since (A), (C), (D) and (E) are incorrect we can eliminate them. Therefore the answer is choice (B).

Important note: (B) is **not** the correct answer simply because it is equal to 9. It is correct because all 4 of the other choices are **not** 9. **You absolutely must check all five choices!**

For more information on this technique, see **Strategy 4** in **"The 32 Most Effective SAT Math Strategies."**

Advanced Method: We can compute the average directly as follows:

    (9 − k + 9 + 9 + k)/3 = 27/3 = 9, choice (B).

* Quick solution: 9 lies midway between 9 − k and 9 + k. Thus the average is 9, choice (B).

59. The average (arithmetic mean) of 11, 25, and y is 25. What is the value of y ?

    (A) 25
    (B) 36
    (C) 38
    (D) 39
    (E) 67

Beginner Method: We change the average to a sum using the formula

Sum = Average * Number

So, in this case we are averaging 3 numbers. Thus the Number is 3. The Average is given to be 25. Thus, the Sum of the 3 numbers is 25*3 = 75. Since we know that two of the numbers are 11 and 25, the third number is 75 – 11 – 25 = 39, choice (D).

For more information on this technique, see **Strategy 20** in **"The 32 Most Effective SAT Math Strategies."**

* Advanced Method: Since the average is 25, y must be at the same distance from 25 as 11. The distance between 11 and 25 is 25 – 11 = 14. It follows that y = 25 + 14 = 39, choice (D).

15, 17, 3, 19, 2, 5, 22, 36, b

60. If b is the median of the 9 numbers listed above, which of the following could be the value of b ?

    (A) 4
    (B) 8
    (C) 14
    (D) 16
    (E) 18

* Let's list the numbers in increasing order: 2, 3, 5, 15, 17, 19, 22, 36. Note that if b is the median (middle number), then 15 ≤ b ≤ 17. The only answer that qualifies is 16, choice (D).

61. Of the 37 marbles in a jar, the most common color is green. What is the probability that a marble randomly selected from the jar is <u>not</u> green?

(A) $\dfrac{1}{37}$

(B) $\dfrac{5}{37}$

(C) $\dfrac{1}{3}$

(D) $\dfrac{36}{37}$

(E) It cannot be determined from the information given.

* Note that we are not told exactly how many green marbles are in the jar. It is consistent with the problem that there are 30 green marbles in the jar, and the remaining 7 are red. Then the required probability is 7/37. Since this is not an answer choice, the answer must be choice (E).

Remark: The solution above shows that the answer is **either** choice (E) **or** 7/37. Since 7/37 is not an answer choice, the answer is choice (E).

Verification of solution: This is not necessary for the SAT, but it would be nice to just verify that the answer is not 7/37. We can do this easily by noting that it is also consistent with the problem that there are 35 green marbles, and 2 red marbles. This would make the answer 2/37. Since we came up with two distinct answers, there is not enough information given in the problem.

62. The average (arithmetic mean) of eight numbers is 65. If a ninth number, 20, is added to the group, what is the average of the nine numbers?

* We use the formula Sum = Average * Number

At first we are averaging eight numbers. Thus the Number is 8. The Average is given to be 65. It follows that the Sum of the eight numbers is 65*8 = 520.

When we add 20 to the group the sum becomes 520 + 20 = 540. Thus the average of the nine numbers is 540/9 = **60**.

Remark: For the last computation we used the same formula above, but in the following form: Average = Sum/Number

For more information on this technique, see **Strategy 20** in **"The 32 Most Effective SAT Math Strategies."**

63. Three light bulbs are placed into three different lamps. How many different arrangements are possible for three light bulbs of different colors – one white, one red, and one green?

Beginner Method: We list all the possibilities:

white   red   green
white   green   red
red   white   green
red   green   white
green   white   red
green   red   white

We can easily see that there are **6** arrangements.

Remark: When you actually write out this list you should use abbreviations such as "w" for white, "r" for red, and "g" for green. This will save some time.

For more information on this technique, see **Strategy 21** in **"The 32 Most Effective SAT Math Strategies."**

* Advanced Method: We can count the arrangements without actually making a list. There are 3 light bulbs, and we are arranging all 3 of them. So there are $_3P_3$ = 3! = 1*2*3 = **6** arrangements.

Permutations: $_3P_3$ means the number of **permutations** of 3 things taken 3 at a time. In a permutation order matters (as opposed to the **combination** $_3C_3$ where the order does not matter).

$$_3P_3 = 3!/0! = (1*2*3)/1 = 6$$

In general, if n is an integer, then n! = 1*2*3*...*n
If n and k are integers, then $_nP_r = n!/(n-r)!$
0! = 1 by definition.

On the SAT you do **not** need to know these formulas. You can do these computations very quickly on your graphing calculator. For example, to compute $_3P_3$, type 3 into your calculator, then in the **Math** menu scroll over to **Prb** and select **nPr** (or press **2**). Then type 3 and hit **Enter**. You will get an answer of 6.

64. *A* is a set of numbers whose average (arithmetic mean) is 7. *B* is a set that is generated by tripling each number in *A*. What is the average of the numbers in set *B*?

* Let's choose a set A with average 7. The simplest such set is A = {7}. Then B = {21}, and we see that the average of the number(s) in set B is **21**.

Remark: The answer to this question is independent of what you choose set A to be. As another example, if we let A = {6, 8}, then B = {18, 24}, and the average of the numbers in B is (18 + 24)/2 = 42/2 = 21.

For the advanced student: Here is a complete rigorous solution (this is certainly **not** recommended for use during the SAT). Let A = {$a_1, a_2,...,a_n$}. We are given that the average of the numbers in A is 7. Therefore the sum of the numbers in A is 7n. That is

$$a_1 + a_2 +...+ a_n = 7n$$

B = {$3a_1, 3a_2,...,3a_n$}. Thus, the sum of the numbers in B is

$$3a_1 + 3a_2 +...+ 3a_n = 3(a_1 + a_2 +...+ a_n) = 3*7n = 21n.$$

Finally, we get the average of the numbers in B by dividing 21n by n to get 21n/n = **21**.

LEVEL 3: NUMBER THEORY

65. If an integer n is divisible by 3, 5, 15, and 25, what is the next larger integer divisible by these numbers?

   (A) $n+15$
   (B) $n+50$
   (C) $n+75$
   (D) $n+125$
   (E) $n+150$

Beginner Method: Let's choose a value of n satisfying the given condition. Multiply the given numbers together to get n = 5625. Starting with choice (A) plug in 5625 for n, and divide the result by each of the given four numbers.

   (A) 5625 + 15 = 5640 (not divisible by 25 since 5640/25 = 225.6)
   (B) 5625 + 50 = 5675 (not divisible by 3 since 5675/3 ~ 1891.67)
   (C) 5625 + 75 = 5700 (divisible by all 3)

Since (C) works we can stop here and choose answer choice (C).

For more information on this technique, see **Strategy 4** in **"The 32 Most Effective SAT Math Strategies."** Also relevant to this problem is **Strategy 2**.

Notes:

(a) We only need to check divisibility by 3 and $5^2 = 25$ since these are the highest powers of primes that are factors of the given numbers.
(b) 15 and 25 would work as well (since together they contain the factors 3 and $5^2 = 25$).
(c) A better choice for n is the **least common multiple** of the four given numbers which is $3*5^2 = 75$. In this case we get the following:

   (A) 75 + 15 = 90 (not divisible by 25 since 90/25 = 3.6)
   (B) 75 + 50 = 125 (not divisible by 3 since 125/3 ~ 41.67)
   (C) 75 + 75 = 150 (divisible by all 3)

Advanced Method: As stated in note (c), the least common multiple of the given numbers is 75. We can therefore add any multiple of 75 to n and maintain divisibility by each of the 4 given numbers. So (C) is the correct answer.

Note: Choice (E) also always gives an integer divisible by the given 4 numbers. It is not correct because it is not the **next** larger integer.

Remarks for the more advanced student:

(a) Here is a quick way to find the least common multiple of a set of positive integers (we will use the 4 integers in the problem as an example).

Step 1: Find the prime factorization of each number in the set.

$$3 = 3$$
$$5 = 5$$
$$15 = 3*5$$
$$25 = 5^2$$

Step 2: Choose the highest power of each prime that appears in any of the factorizations.

$$3 \text{ and } 5^2$$

Step 3: Multiply these numbers together to get the least common multiple.

$$3*5^2 = 75$$

(b) Note that if n is divisible by 75 it can be written as 75k for some integer k. Thus n + 75 = 75k + 75 = 75(k + 1). So n + 75 is divisible by 75, and thus by any factor of 75 including 3, 5, 15 and 25.

Remark: Now that we know the above theory we see that we can get the next larger number divisible by the given numbers by adding the lcm of the given numbers.

* **Quick Solution:** lcm = $3*5^2$ = 75. So the answer is n + 75, choice (C).

$$2C$$
$$+ \quad C$$
$$\overline{\quad 3D \quad}$$

66. In the correctly solved addition problem above, C and D represent digits. If C is not equal to D, how many different digits from 0 through 9 could C represent?

    (A) Three
    (B) Four
    (C) Five
    (D) Six
    (E) Seven

* In the worst case we simply need to do 10 simple addition problems (by plugging in each of 0 through 9 for C). Let's try to minimize the number of computations we need to do. If we set C equal to 4, then we get 24 + 4 = 28. From this computation we see that C must be at least 5. Now, 25 + 5 = 30, 26 + 6 = 32, 27 + 7 = 34, 28 + 8 = 36, 29 + 9 = 38. So there are 5 possibilities for C, and the answer is choice (C).

Note: We need to be careful to actually do all 5 of those computations to make sure that C is not equal to D in each case.

67. How many <u>seconds</u> are required for a bicycle to go 2 miles at a constant speed of 4 miles per hour?

    (A) 3600
    (B) 3000
    (C) 2400
    (D) 1800
    (E) 1200

* At 4 miles per hour it will take a half hour to go 2 miles. A half hour is 30 minutes. There are 60 seconds in each minute. So 30*60 = 1800 seconds. Thus, the answer is choice (D).

Formal solution using d = r*t: We are given d = 2 and r = 4. So

$$t = d/r = 2/4 = .5 \text{ hrs.}$$

To change to seconds we multiply by 3600. So .5*3600 = 1800 seconds, choice (D).

68. The cost of 5 shirts is d dollars. At this rate, what is the cost, in dollars of 45 shirts?

　　(A) $\dfrac{9d}{5}$

　　(B) $\dfrac{d}{45}$

　　(C) $\dfrac{45}{d}$

　　(D) $9d$

　　(E) $45d$

We will use the technique of **picking numbers**. Let's choose a value for d that is relatively simple, but not too simple. A nice choice is d = 10. So 5 shirts cost 10 dollars, and therefore 45 shirts cost 10*9 = **90** dollars. Put a nice big, dark circle around this number so that you can find it easily later. We now substitute 10 in for d into **all** five answer choices.

　　(A) 90/5 = 18
　　(B) 10/45
　　(C) 45/10 = 4.5
　　(D) 9*10 = 90
　　(E) 45*10 = 450

Since (D) is the only choice that has become 90, we conclude that (D) is the answer.

Important note: (D) is **not** the correct answer simply because it is equal to 90. It is correct because all 4 of the other choices are **not** 90.

For more information on this technique, see **Strategy 4** in **"The 32 Most Effective SAT Math Strategies."**

* **Another method using ratios:** We begin by identifying 2 key words. In this case, such a pair of key words is "shirts" and "dollars."

shirts	5	45
dollars	d	x

Notice that we wrote in the number of shirts next to the word shirts, and the cost of the shirts next to the word dollars. Also notice that the cost for 5 shirts is written under the number 5, and the (unknown) cost for 45 shirts is written under the 45. Now draw in the division symbols and equal sign, cross multiply and divide the corresponding ratio to find the unknown quantity x.

$$5/d = 45/x$$
$$5x = 45d$$
$$x = 9d$$

So 45 shirts cost 9d dollars, choice (D).

For more information on this technique, see **Strategy 14** in **"The 32 Most Effective SAT Math Strategies."**

69. Which of the following is equal to $\dfrac{m+50}{10}$?

(A) $\dfrac{m}{10} + 5$

(B) $m + 5$

(C) $5m$

(D) $\dfrac{m+25}{5}$

(E) $\dfrac{m+5}{5}$

Beginner Method: We will use the technique of **picking numbers**. Let's choose a value for m that is relatively simple, say m = 20. We first substitute a 20 in for m into the given expression and use our calculator.

We type in the following: (20 + 50)/10 and get m = **7**. Put a nice big, dark circle around this number so that you can find it easily later. We now substitute a 20 into each answer choice and use our calculator.

(A) 20/10 + 5 = 7
(B) 20 + 5 = 25
(C) 5*20 = 100
(D) (20 + 25)/5 = 9
(E) (20 + 5)/5 = 5

We now compare each of these numbers to the number that we put a nice big, dark circle around. Since (B), (C), (D) and (E) are incorrect we can eliminate them. Therefore the answer is choice (A).

Important note: (A) is **not** the correct answer simply because it is equal to 7. It is correct because all 4 of the other choices are **not** 7. **You absolutely must check all five choices!**

For more information on this technique, see **Strategy 4** in **"The 32 Most Effective SAT Math Strategies."**

Advanced Method: Most students have no trouble at all adding two fractions with the same denominator. For example,

$$m/10 + 50/10 = (m + 50)/10$$

But these same students have trouble reversing this process.

$$(m + 50)/10 = m/10 + 50/10$$

Note that these two equations are **identical** except that the left and right hand sides have been switched. Note also that to break a fraction into two (or more) pieces, the original denominator is repeated for **each** piece.

* Thus an algebraic solution to the above problem consists of the following simple computation.

$$(m + 50)/10 = m/10 + 50/10 = m/10 + 5$$

This is choice (A).

70. What percent of 70 is 14? (Disregard the percent symbol when gridding in your answer.)

* The word "what" indicates an unknown, let's call it x. The word percent means "out of 100" or "divided by 100." The word "of" indicates multiplication, and the word "is" indicates an equal sign. So we translate the given sentence into an algebraic equation as follows.

$$x/100 * 70 = 14$$

So x = 14*100/70 = **20**.

71. When the positive integer x is divided by 6, the remainder is 2. What is the remainder when $x + 21$ is divided by 6?

Let's choose a positive integer whose remainder is 2 when it is divided by 6. A simple way to find such an x is to add 6 and 2. So let x = 8. It follows that x + 21 = 8 + 21 = 29. 6 goes into 29 four times with a remainder of **5**.

Important: To find a remainder you must perform division **by hand**. Dividing in your calculator does **not** give you a remainder!

See p. 53 in **"The 32 Most Effective SAT Math Strategies"** for a calculator algorithm that simulates long division and gets you these remainders very quickly.

Note: A slightly simpler choice for x is x = 2. Indeed, when 2 is divided by 6 we get 0 with 2 left over. Since this choice for x sometimes confuses students I decided to use 6 + 2 = 8 which is the next simplest choice. Note that in general we can get a value for x by starting with any multiple of 6 and adding 2. So x = 6n + 2 for some integer n.

* Quickest solution: Let x = 2. It follows that x + 21 = 2 + 21 = 23. 6 goes into 23 three times with a remainder of **5**.

Remark: The answer to this problem is independent of our choice for x

70

(assuming that x satisfies the given condition, of course). The method just described does **not** show this. It is not necessary to do so.

For more information on this technique, see **Strategy 4** in **"The 32 Most Effective SAT Math Strategies."**

For the advanced student: Here is a complete algebraic solution that actually demonstrates the independence of choice for x. The given condition means that we can write x as x = 6n + 2 for some integer n. Then

x + 21 = (6n + 2) + 21 = 6n + 23 = 6n + 18 + 5 = 6(n + 3) + 5 = 6z + 5

where z is the integer n + 3. This shows that when x + 21 is divided by 6 the remainder is **5**.

72.   The quantity (4×6^9) is how many times the quantity (4×6^5) ?

Beginner Method: Simply divide the two numbers in your calculator. Type it in your calculator **exactly** like this:

(4*6^9)/(4*6^5)

The answer is **1296**.

* Advanced Method: $4*6^9 = (4*6^5)*6^4$. So the answer is 6^4 = **1296**.

See p. 57 in **"The 32 Most Effective SAT Math Strategies"** for a summary of the basic exponent laws that you should know for the SAT.

LEVEL 3: ALGEBRA AND FUNCTIONS

73. A group of x children has collected 40 playing cards. If each child collects y more playing cards per week for the next w weeks, which of the following represents the number of playing cards that will be in the group's collection?

    (A) $40xy$

    (B) $40 + \dfrac{wy}{x}$

    (C) $40 + \dfrac{wx}{y}$

    (D) $40 + xy + w$

    (E) $40 + wxy$

Beginner Method: We will use the technique of **picking numbers**. Let's try the numbers x = 5, y = 2 and w = 3. Then 5 children collected 40 cards. Each child collects 2 more cards per week for 3 weeks. That's 5*2*3 = 30 more cards for a total of **70** cards. We now substitute the numbers we chose into each answer choice.

    (A) 40*5*2 = 400
    (B) 40 + 3*2/5 = 41.2
    (C) 40 + 3*5/2 = 47.5
    (D) 40 + 5*2 + 3 = 53
    (E) 40 + 3*5*2 = 70

Since (A), (B), (C) and (D) are incorrect we can eliminate them. Therefore the answer is choice (E).

Important note: (E) is **not** the correct answer simply because it is equal to 70. It is correct because all four of the other choices are **not** 70.

Remark: It is not necessary to finish a computation if the answer is clearly incorrect. For example, in choice (B) we could stop at 40 + 3*2/5 since this is clearly not an integer, and the answer is an integer.

For more information on this technique, see **Strategy 4** in **"The 32 Most Effective SAT Math Strategies."**

* **Advanced Method: (**x children)*(y cards)*(w weeks) = xyw additional cards. Adding this amount to the original 40 gives us answer choice (E).

74. If $15x + 55y = 35$, what is the value of $3x + 11y$?

    (A) 7
    (B) 8
    (C) 14
    (D) 15
    (E) 30

* We divide both sides of the equation by 5 to get 3x + 11y = 7, choice (A).

Note: When we divide the left hand side by 5, we have to divide **each** term by 5.

    15x/5 = 3x   55y/5 = 11y

Alternative: We can factor out 5 on the left hand side

    15x + 55y = 5(3x + 11y).

So we have

$$15x + 55y = 35$$
$$5(3x + 11y) = 35$$
$$3x + 11y = 7.$$

This is choice (A).

For more information on this technique, see **Strategy 16** in **"The 32 Most Effective SAT Math Strategies."**

75. The function k is defined by $k(x) = 2x^2 + bx - 3$, where b is a constant. In the xy-plane, the graph of $y = k(x)$ crosses the x-axis where $x = 3$. What is the value of b?

    (A) 5
    (B) 3
    (C) 0
    (D) -3
    (E) -5

* A graph crosses the x-axis at a point where $y = 0$. Thus, the point (3, 0) is on the graph of y = k(x). Equivalently, k(3) = 0. So

$$0 = 2*3^2 + 3b - 3$$
$$0 = 2*9 + 3b - 3$$
$$0 = 18 + 3b - 3$$
$$0 = 15 + 3b$$
$$3b = -15$$
$$b = -15/3 = -5, \text{ choice (E)}.$$

	4			4
	$4a$			$2a$
	8			8
	b			c
	+9			+9
	41			26

76. In the correctly worked addition problems above, what is the value of $2a + b - c$?

    (A) 14
    (B) 15
    (C) 16
    (D) 17
    (E) 18

Beginner Method: If we choose any value for a, then b and c will be determined. So, let's set a equal to 0. Then

$$4 + 8 + b + 9 = 41$$
$$21 + b = 41$$
$$b = 20$$

and

$$4 + 8 + c + 9 = 26$$
$$21 + c = 26$$
$$c = 5$$

So $2a + b - c = 0 + 20 - 5 = 15$, choice (B).

Remark: Any choice for a will give us the same answer. We could have chosen a value for b or c as well. But once we choose a value for one of the variables the other two are determined.

For more information on this technique, see **Strategy 4** in **"The 32 Most Effective SAT Math Strategies."**

Advanced Method: Let's rewrite the equations horizontally since that is how most of us are used to seeing equations.

$$4 + 4a + 8 + b + 9 = 41$$
$$4 + 2a + 8 + c + 9 = 26$$

We now use a simple operation. The operation to use here is subtraction. Let's go ahead and subtract term by term.

$$4 + 4a + 8 + b + 9 = 41$$
$$\underline{4 + 2a + 8 + c + 9 = 26}$$
$$2a + (b - c) = 15$$

Thus, the answer is choice (B).

Remark: Whenever we are trying to find an expression that involves addition, subtraction, or both, **adding or subtracting** the given equations usually does the trick.

For more information on this technique, see **Strategy 16** in **"The 32 Most Effective SAT Math Strategies."**

* **Visualizing the answer:** You can save a substantial amount of time by performing the subtraction in your head (left equation minus right equation). Note that above the lines the subtraction yields 2a + b − c. This is exactly what we're looking for. Thus, we need only subtract below the lines to get the answer: 41 − 26 = **15**.

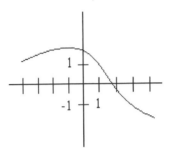

77. The figure above shows the graph of the function f. Which of the following is greater than $f(-2)$?

   (A) $f(-4)$
   (B) $f(-3)$
   (C) $f(-1)$
   (D) $f(1)$
   (E) $f(2)$

* Let's draw a horizontal line through the point (-2, f(-2)). To do this start on the x-axis at -2 and go straight up until you hit the curve. This height is f(-2). Now draw a horizontal line through this point.

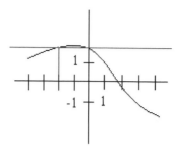

Now, notice that the graph is above this line when x = -1. So f(-1) is greater than f(-2). Therefore the answer is choice (C).

78. If $\dfrac{x}{y} = \dfrac{3}{r}$, then $\dfrac{y}{xr} =$

* We begin by cross multiplying.

$$x/y = 3/r$$
$$xr = 3y$$

We then divide both sides by y to get xr/y = 3

Finally, we take the reciprocal of both sides to get

$$y/xr = \mathbf{1/3}.$$

We can also grid in the decimal **.333**.

Solution by picking numbers: Let's plug in values for x, y and r. Let's try the following.

$$r = 6 \quad x = 2 \quad y = 4.$$

Notice that we chose the numbers so that the given equation holds. The answer is then y/xr = 4/(2*6) = .33333333. So we can grid in **.333** or **1/3**.

79. Let g be a function such that $g(x) = |2x| + k$ where k is a constant. If $g(3) = -2$, what is the value of $g(-5)$?

* g(3) = |2*3| + k = 6 + k. But it is given that g(3) = -2. So 6 + k = -2, and therefore k = -8. So g(x) = |2x| - 8. Finally,

$$g(-5) = |2(-5)| - 8 = |-10| - 8 = 10 - 8 = \textbf{2.}$$

Recall: |x| is the **absolute value** of x. If x is nonnegative, then |x| = x. If x is negative, then |x| = -x (in other words, if x is negative, then taking the absolute value just eliminates the minus sign). For example, |10| = 10 and |-10| = 10.

80. If $(\dfrac{x^2 + 3}{y^3 + 2}) = \dfrac{3}{5}$, what does $(\dfrac{2 + y^3}{3 + x^2})^2$ equal?

* Taking the reciprocal of the given equation yields

$$(y^3 + 2)/(x^2 + 3) = 5/3.$$

This is the same as $(2 + y^3)/(3 + x^2) = 5/3$.

Squaring both sides of this equation gives us **25/9**.

Remarks:

(1) We can also grid this as one of the decimals **2.77** or **2.78**.

(2) The expression $(x^2 + 3)/(y^3 + 2)$ can be thought of as a **block**.

For more information on blocks, see **Strategy 19** in **"The 32 Most Effective SAT Math Strategies."**

LEVEL 3: GEOMETRY

81. The volume of a right circular cylinder is 125π cubic centimeters. If the height and base radius of the cylinder are equal, what is the base radius of the cylinder?

   (A) 3 centimeters
   (B) 5 centimeters
   (C) 7 centimeters
   (D) 15 centimeters
   (E) 25 centimeters

Let's start with choice (C) as our first guess. We are guessing that r = 7. Thus h = 7 too. So V = $\pi r^2 h$ = $\pi(7)^2(7)$ = 343π. This is too big so that we can eliminate choices (C), (D) and (E). Let's try choice (B) next. Therefore r = h = 5, and V = $\pi r^2 h$ = $\pi(5)^2(5)$ = 125π. This is correct, and so the answer is choice (B).

Remark: Note that the formula for the volume of a cylinder is given to you on the SAT.

For more information on this technique, see **Strategy 1** in **"The 32 Most Effective SAT Math Strategies."**

* **An algebraic solution for the more advanced student:**

$$V = \pi r^2 h$$
$$125\pi = \pi r^2 r$$
$$125 = r^3$$
$$5 = r.$$

Therefore the answer is choice (B).

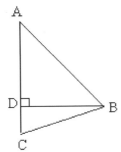

Note: Figure not drawn to scale.

82. Triangle *ABC* has the same area as a rectangle with sides of lengths 5 and 7. If the length of *AC* is 10, what is the length of *BD*?

    (A) 4
    (B) 5
    (C) 6
    (D) 7
    (E) 8

* The area of the rectangle is (5)(7) = 35. Thus the triangle also has area 35. So ½ bh = 35. The base of the triangle has length 10. So ½ *10h = 35, or 5h = 35. Thus h = 7. Since BD is the height of the triangle the answer is choice (D).

Remark: Note that the formulas for the area of a rectangle and the area of a triangle are given to you on the SAT.

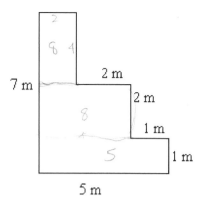

Note: Figure not drawn to scale.

83. What is the area of the figure above?

(A) 15 m^2
(B) 17 m^2
(C) 19 m^2
(D) 21 m^2
(E) 23 m^2

* We break the figure up into 3 rectangles and compute the length and width of each rectangle.

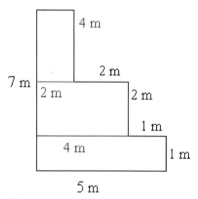

Note: Figure not drawn to scale.

The length and width of the bottom rectangle are 5 and 1 making the area 5*1 = 5 m^2.

The length of the middle rectangle is 5 − 1 = 4, and the width is given as 2. Thus, the area is 4*2 = 8 m^2.

The length of the top rectangle is 4 − 2 = 2, and the width is 7 − 1 − 2 = 4. Thus, the area is 2*4 = 8 m^2.

We then get the total area by adding up the areas of the three rectangles: 5 + 8 + 8 = 21 m^2, choice (D).

Remark: Notice that if we have the full length of a line segment, and one partial length of the same line segment, then we get the other length by subtracting the two given lengths.

84. In the xy-coordinate plane, line n passes through the points (0,2) and (1,0). If line m is perpendicular to line n, what is the slope of line m ?

   (A) - 2
   (B) $-\dfrac{1}{2}$
   (C) 1
   (D) $\dfrac{1}{2}$
   (E) 2

* We first compute the slope of line n. We can do this by plotting the two points, and computing rise/run = -2/1 (to get from (0,2) to (1,0) we go down 2 and right 1). Since line m is perpendicular to line n, the slope of line m is the negative reciprocal of the slope of line n. So the answer is 1/2, choice (D).

Remark: We can also find the slope of line n by using the slope formula m = $(y_2 − y_1)/(x_2 − x_1)$ = (0 − 2)/(1 − 0) = -2/1 = -2.

For more information on this technique, see **Strategy 28** in **"The 32 Most Effective SAT Math Strategies."**

85. Point O lies in plane P. How many circles are there in plane P that have center O and an area of 16π centimeters?

    (A) None
    (B) One
    (C) Two
    (D) Three
    (E) More than three

* Since the area of the circle is 16π, the radius is 4. Once the center and radius of a circle are given, the circle is uniquely determined. Therefore the answer is One, choice (B).

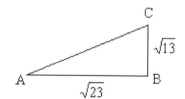

Note: Figure not drawn to scale.

86. In right triangle ABC above, what is the length of side AC?

* We use the Pythagorean Theorem: $c^2 = a^2 + b^2 = 23 + 13 = 36$. Therefore $AC = c = $ **6**.

Note: The Pythagorean Theorem is one of the formulas given to you in the beginning of each math section.

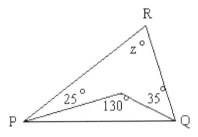

Note: Figure not drawn to scale.

87. In triangle *PQR* above, what is the value of *z* ?

Beginner Method: Since every triangle has 180 degrees we choose values for the angle measures of the small triangle that add up to 180 − 130 = 50, say 25 and 25.

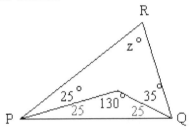

Note: Figure not drawn to scale.

We now see that z = 180 − 25 − 25 − 35 − 25 = **70**.

Remark: We could have chosen **any** two numbers that add up to 50 for the angles of the small triangle.

* Advanced Method: The two unlabeled angles in the smaller triangle must add up to 50. Therefore

$$z = 180 - 25 - 35 - 50 = \textbf{70}.$$

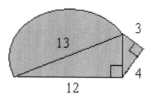

88. What is the total area of the shaded region above to the nearest integer?

* Note that the side not labeled in the picture has length 5. To see this you can use either of the Pythagorean triples 3, 4, 5, or 5, 12, 13. If you don't remember these triples you can use the Pythagorean Theorem:

$$c^2 = 3^2 + 4^2 = 9 + 16 = 25. \text{ So } c = 5.$$

or

$$13^2 = 12^2 + b^2. \text{ So } 169 = 144 + b^2, \text{ and } b^2 = 25. \text{ Thus, } b = 5.$$

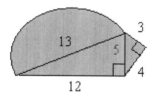

Recall that the area of a triangle is A = ½ bh.

Thus, the area of the smaller triangle is ½ 3*4 = 6.

The area of the larger triangle is ½ 12*5 = 30.

Recall also that the area of a circle is πr^2. Thus, the area of the given semicircle is ½ $\pi(13/2)^2$ = $(169/8)\pi$ ~ 66.36614481 = 66 to the nearest integer.

Therefore the total area to the nearest integer is 6 + 30 + 66 = **102**.

LEVEL 3: PROBABILITY AND STATISTICS

89. The average (arithmetic mean) of seven numbers is 10. When an eighth number is added, the average of the eight numbers is also 10. What is the eighth number?

  (A) 0
  (B) $\dfrac{4}{5}$
  (C) $\dfrac{5}{4}$
  (D) 8
  (E) 10

We change the averages to sums using the formula

$$\text{Sum} = \text{Average} * \text{Number}$$

The sum of the seven numbers is 10*7 = 70.
The sum of the eight numbers is 10*8 = 80.
The eighth number is 80 − 70 = 10, choice (E).

Note: The above formula comes from eliminating the denominator in the definition of average.

$$\text{Average} = \text{Sum/Number}$$

For more information on this technique, see **Strategy 20** in **"The 32 Most Effective SAT Math Strategies."**

* **Quick solution:** The only way to add a number to a list without changing the average is to add the average itself. So the answer is 10, choice (E).

A complete algebraic solution for the advanced student: This method is **not** recommended for the SAT, but it is included for completeness. Let x be the sum of the first seven numbers, and let y be the eighth number. We are given that x/7 = 10 and (x + y)/8 = 10. From the first equation it is

86

easy to see that x = 70 (by multiplying both sides of the equation by 7). Now we substitute 70 in for x in the second equation and solve for y.

(70 + y)/8 = 10. So 70 + y = 80. Therefore y = 10, choice (E).

90. In a survey, 62 cat owners were asked about two brands of cat food, Brand X and Brand Y. Of the people surveyed, 26 used Brand X, 11 used Brand Y, and 4 used both brands. How many of the people surveyed didn't use either brand of cat food?

    (A) 15
    (B) 26
    (C) 27
    (D) 28
    (E) 29

* Total = X + Y − Both + Neither.

Total = 62, X = 26, Y = 11, and Both = 4.

62 = 26 + 11 − 4 + Neither = 33 + Neither.

Therefore, Neither = 62 − 33 = 29, choice (E).

Alternate solution using a Venn diagram: We draw a Venn diagram

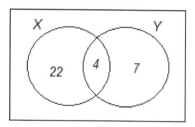

Note that when we draw the diagram we begin with the intersection. This is given to be 4. 26 − 4 = 22, and 11 − 4 = 7. Finally,

62 − 22 − 4 − 7 = 29, choice (E).

91. A chemist is testing 5 different liquids. For each test, the chemist chooses 3 of the liquids and mixes them together. What is the least number of tests that must be done so that every possible combination of liquids is tested?

    (A) 5
    (B) 10
    (C) 15
    (D) 20
    (E) 25

* This is a **combination**. The answer is $_5C_3 = 10$, choice (B).

Remarks:

(1) This is a combination because it does not matter what order we take the three liquids. We are simply grabbing three of them and mixing them together.

(2) We can compute $_5C_3$ very quickly on our calculator as follows: first type 5. Then under the Math menu scroll over to PRB and select nCr. Finally type 3 and press ENTER.

(3) The formula for $_nC_r$ is $n!/[r!(n-r)!]$. So $_5C_3 = 5!/(3!2!) = (5)(4)/2 = 10$. (Note that this is included for completeness. You do not need to know this formula.)

A solution using a list: We can also solve this problem by simply listing all of the possibilities. In the following list a * means we are choosing that liquid, and an O means we are not:

***OO	*OO**
**O*O	O***O
**OO*	O**O*
*O**O	O*O**
*O*O*	OO***

For more information on this technique, see **Strategy 21** in **"The 32 Most Effective SAT Math Strategies."**

92. There are y bricks in a row. If one brick is to be selected at random, the probability that it will be cracked is $\dfrac{5}{7}$. In terms of y, how many of the bricks are cracked?

(A) $\dfrac{y}{7}$

(B) $\dfrac{5y}{7}$

(C) $\dfrac{7y}{5}$

(D) $\dfrac{12y}{7}$

(E) $7y$

Let's choose a value for y, say y = 7. Then there are 7 bricks in a row. Since the probability is 5/7 that a brick is cracked, 5 of the bricks are cracked. Put a nice, big dark circle around the number **5**. We now substitute 7 in for y in each of the answer choices.

(A) 1
(B) 5
(C) 49/5
(D) 12
(E) 49

Since (A), (C), (D) and (E) are incorrect we can eliminate them. Therefore the answer is choice (B).

Important note: (B) is **not** the correct answer simply because it is equal to 5. It is correct because all 4 of the other choices are **not** 5.

For more information on this technique, see **Strategy 4 in "The 32 Most Effective SAT Math Strategies."**

An algebraic solution for the more advanced student: Let x be the number of cracked bricks. Then x/y=5/7. Now cross multiply and divide to solve for x.

7x = 5y, and thus x = 5y/7, choice (B).

*Quick solution: We are given that 5/7 of the total number of bricks is cracked. The total is y, so that the answer is (5/7)*y = 5y/7, choice (B).

TEST GRADES OF STUDENTS IN MATH CLASS

Test Grade	75	82	87	93	100
Number of students with that grade	5	7	10	3	1

93. The test grades of the 26 students in a math class are shown in the chart above. What is the median test grade for the class?

   (A) 75
   (B) 82
   (C) 87
   (D) 90
   (E) 93

Let's list the test grades in increasing order, including repetitions.

75, 75, 75, 75, 75, 82, 82, 82, 82, 82, 82, 82, 87, 87, 87, 87, 87, 87, 87, 87, 87, 87, 93, 93, 93, 100

Now strike off two numbers at a time simultaneously, one from each end until just two numbers are left.

~~75, 75, 75, 75, 75, 82, 82, 82, 82, 82, 82, 82,~~ 87, 87, ~~87, 87, 87, 87, 87, 87, 87, 87, 93, 93, 93, 100~~

Note that there are two 87's left. The average of 87 and 87 is 87, choice (C).

* Doing it in your head: You can do this problem very quickly without writing anything down. If we "strike off" all 5 of the 75s, then we should "strike off" the 100, the three 93s, and one of the 87s. So there are nine 87s and the seven 82s left. Since there are more 87s, the median is 87, choice (C).

94. Set A contains only the integers 0 through 99 inclusive. If a number is selected at random from A, what is the probability that the number selected will be greater than 79?

* There are a total of 100 integers. There are 100 − 80 = 20 integers greater than 79. Therefore the probability is 20/ 100 = **1/5** or **.2**.

Remark: The number of integers from a to b is **b − a + 1**. So in this example, the number of integers from 80 to 99 is

$$99 - 80 + 1 = 100 - 80 = 20.$$

95. Marco and eight other students took two exams, and each exam yielded an integer grade for each student. The two grades for each student were added together. The sum of these two grades for each of the nine students was 142, 153, 140, 120, 142, 111, 180, 114, and Marco's sum, which was the median of the nine sums. If Marco's first test grade was 65, what is one possible grade Marco could have received on the second test?

* Let's begin by writing the sums in increasing order.

$$111, 114, 120, 140, 142, 142, 153, 180$$

Since Marco's sum is the median, it is 140, 141 or 142. Let's pick one, say 141. Since Marco's first test grade was 65, his second test grade was 141− 65 = **76**.

Remark: The other two choices yield the answers

$$140 - 65 = 75 \text{ or } 142 - 65 = 77.$$

So you can grid in **75, 76,** or **77**.

96. Six different books are to be stacked in a pile. One book is chosen for the bottom of the pile. In how many different orders can the remaining books be placed on the stack?

There are five books left to stack. Thus there are 5! = 5*4*3*2*1 = **120** ways to stack these books.

LEVEL 4: NUMBER THEORY

97. A positive integer is called a palindrome if it reads the same forward as it does backward. For example, 2442 is a palindrome. The next two palindromes greater than 71817 are x and y, where $x < y$. What is the value of $y - x$?

   (A) 10
   (B) 90
   (C) 100
   (D) 110
   (E) 210

* The next two palindromes are x = 71917 and y = 72027. So we have that y − x = 72027 − 71917 = 110. Thus the answer is choice (D).

98. Set A consists of k integers, and the difference between the greatest integer in A and the least integer in A is 850. A new set of k integers, set B, is formed by multiplying each integer in A by 4 and then adding 10 to the product. What is the difference between the greatest integer in B and the least integer in B?

   (A) 800
   (B) 850
   (C) 860
   (D) 3400
   (E) 3410

* The question implies that any choice for k will produce the same answer. So, let's choose k = 2, and let A = {0, 850}. Then B = {10, 3410},

and the difference between the greatest and least integer in B is

$$3410 - 10 = 3400.$$

Thus, the answer is choice (D).

We used **Strategy 4** in **"The 32 Most Effective SAT Math Strategies."**

An algebraic solution for the advanced student: Let x and y be the least and greatest integers in set A, respectively. Then the least and greatest integers in set B are 4x + 10 and 4y + 10. So the difference between the greatest and least integer in B is

$$(4y + 10) - (4x + 10) = 4y + 10 - 4x - 10 = 4y - 4x = 4(y - x) = 4*850 \,.$$

Since 4*850 = 3400 the answer is choice (D).

Caution: A common mistake is to distribute the minus sign incorrectly. The following computation is **wrong**.

$$(4y + 10) - (4x + 10) = 4y + 10 - 4x + 10$$

Quasi-elimination note: We can quasi-eliminate (A) and (E) because the word least (or greatest) appears in the question. We can quasi-eliminate (B) because the number 850 is in the question. See **Strategy 10** in **"The 32 Most Effective SAT Math Strategies"** for a detailed explanation of this technique.

99. The sum of 12 positive even integers is 46. Some of these integers are equal to each other. What is the greatest possible value of one of these integers?

    (A) 26
    (B) 24
    (C) 22
    (D) 20
    (E) 18

* To make one of the integers as large as possible we will make the other eleven as small as possible. The smallest even positive integer is 2, so we make 11 of the integers 2. Thus the 12th integer is

$$46 - 11*2 = 46 - 22 = 24.$$

Thus the answer is choice (B).

In this problem we have used **Strategy 32** in **"The 32 Most Effective SAT Math Strategies."**

Note: Since the word greatest appears and this is a Level 4 problem we can quasi-eliminate choices (A) and (E). So if we were to guess we would choose between (B), (C) and (D). See **Strategy 10** in **"The 32 Most Effective SAT Math Strategies"** for a detailed explanation of this technique.

100. A person cuts a cake into n equal pieces and eats two pieces. In terms of n, what percent of the cake is left?

(A) $100(n-2)\,\%$

(B) $\dfrac{100(n-2)}{n}\,\%$

(C) $\dfrac{100n}{n-2}\,\%$

(D) $\dfrac{n-2}{100}\,\%$

(E) $\dfrac{n-2}{100n}\,\%$

* We will use the technique of **picking numbers**. Let's choose a value for n, say n = 100 (the number 100 is often a good choice in percent problems – after all, the word percent means "out of 100"). So the person eats 2 pieces of the cake and there are 98 left. Since there were 100 pieces total, the answer is **98%**. We now substitute our chosen value of n into each answer choice.

(A) 100*98 = 9800%
(B) 100*98/100 = 98%
(C) 100*100/98 =~ 102.04 %
(D) 98/100 = 0.98%
(E) 98/(100*100) = 0.0098%

Since (A), (C), (D) and (E) are incorrect we can eliminate them. Therefore the answer is choice (B).

For more information on this technique, see **Strategy 4** in **"The 32 Most Effective SAT Math Strategies."**

* An algebraic solution for the advanced student: The total number of pieces of cake is n. Since 2 bricks have been eaten, it follows that n − 2 have not been eaten. To get the **fraction** of cake that has not been eaten we divide the **number** of pieces that have not been eaten by the total. This is (n − 2)/n. To change this to a **percent** we multiply by 100, to get 100(n − 2)/n %, choice (B).

Note: The last step in the algebraic solution is equivalent to the usual ratio computation where we are changing the denominator to 100.

pieces not eaten   n − 2   x
total no. of pieces   n   100

$$(n - 2)/n = x/100$$
$$100(n - 2) = nx$$
$$100(n - 2)/n = x$$

For more information on this technique, see **Strategy 14** in **"The 32 Most Effective SAT Math Strategies."**

101. If k, m, and n are distinct positive integers such that n is divisible by m, and m is divisible by k, which of the following statements must be true?

  I. n is divisible by k.
  II. $n = mk$.
  III. n has more than 2 positive factors.

(A) I only
(B) III only
(C) I and II only
(D) I and III only
(E) I, II, and III

* Let's pick some numbers. Let k = 3, m = 15, and n = 30. Then n is divisible by m, and m is divisible by k. Let's look at each roman numeral now.

  I. 30 is divisible by 3. True.
  II. 30 = 15*3 is False.
  III. the factors of 30 are 1, 2, 3, 5, 6, 10, 15, and 30. True.

Since II is false we can eliminate choices (C) and (E). Answer choice (D) would be a good guess at this point. There are now 2 ways to complete this problem:

Method 1: Pick another set of numbers and verify that I and III are still true. This will give more evidence that choice (D) is correct, thus making choice (D) the best guess.

Method 2 (advanced): Let's show that I and III always hold under the given conditions.

Let's start with I: Since n is divisible by m, there is an integer b such that n = bm. Since m is divisible by k, there is an integer c such that m = ck. Thus, n = bm = b(ck) = (bc)k. Since bc is an integer it follows that n is divisible by k.

And now III: Since n is divisible by m, m is a factor of n. We also just showed that n is divisible by k. So k is a factor of n. Also, every integer is a factor of itself. Thus n is a factor of n. So k, m, and n are 3 factors of n. The problem tells us they are distinct.

Therefore the answer is choice (D).

102. A positive integer is called a palindrome if it reads the same forward as it does backward. For example, 2442 is a palindrome. How many three-digit palindromes are there?

* Once we choose the first digit the last digit is determined (the last digit must be the same as the first digit). There are 9 choices for the first digit (1 through 9) and 10 choices for the second digit (0 through 9). So all together there are 9*10 = **90**.

103. If k is divided by 9, the remainder is 4. What is the remainder if $3k$ is divided by 9?

Let's choose a positive integer whose remainder is 4 when it is divided by 9. A simple way to find such a k is to add 9 and 4. So let k = 13. It follows that 3k = 3*13 = 39. 9 goes into 39 four times with a remainder of **3**.

Important: To find a remainder you must perform division **by hand**. Dividing in your calculator does **not** give you a remainder!

See p. 51 in **"The 32 Most Effective SAT Math Strategies"** for a calculator algorithm that simulates long division and gets you these remainders very quickly.

* **Quickest solution:** A slightly simpler choice for k is k = 4. Indeed, when 4 is divided by 9 we get 0 with 4 left over. Then 3k = 12, and the remainder when 12 is divided by 9 is **3**.

Note that in general we can get a value for k by starting with any multiple of 9 and adding 4. So k = 9n + 4 for some integer n.

For more information on this technique, see **Strategy 4** in **"The 32 Most Effective SAT Math Strategies."**

Remark: The answer to this problem is independent of our choice for k (assuming that k satisfies the given condition, of course). The method just described does **not** show this. That is not our concern however.

For the advanced student: Here is a complete algebraic solution that actually demonstrates the independence of choice for k. The given condition means that we can write k as $k = 9n + 4$ for some integer n. Then

$$3k = 3(9n + 4) = 27n + 12 = 9(3n + 1) + 3 = 9z + 3$$

where z is the integer $3n + 1$. This shows that when 3k is divided by 9 the remainder is 3.

104. A mixture is made by combining a red liquid and a blue liquid so that the ratio of the red liquid to the blue liquid is 17 to 3 by weight. How many liters of the blue liquid are needed to make a 420 liter mixture?

* We can represent the number of liters of red liquid by 17x and the number of liters of blue liquid by 3x for some number x. Then the total amount of liquid is 20x which must be equal to 420. $20x = 420$ implies that $x = 21$. Since we want the number of liters of blue liquid, we need to find 3x. This is $3(21) = $ **63**.

Important note: After you find x make sure you look at what the question is asking for. A common error is to give an answer of 21. But the amount of blue liquid is **not** equal to x. It is equal to 3x!

Alternate solution: We set up a ratio of the amount of blue liquid to the total liquid.

blue liquid	3	x
total liquid	20	420

$$3/20 = x/420$$
$$20x = 3*420$$
$$x = 3*420/20 = \textbf{63}.$$

For more information on this technique, see **Strategy 14** in **"The 32 Most Effective SAT Math Strategies."**

LEVEL 4: ALGEBRA AND FUNCTIONS

105. If $x^2 = 9$ and $y^2 = 5$, then $(2x + y)^2$ could equal which of the following?

   (A) 41
   (B) 61
   (C) 121
   (D) $61 - 12\sqrt{5}$
   (E) $41 + 12\sqrt{5}$

* Taking positive square roots in our calculator gives x = 3 and y ~ 2.236. Substituting into the given expression we get (2*3 + 2.236)² ~ 67.832. Let's see if choice (E) matches with this. We put the number in choice (E) in our calculator to get approximately 67.832. Thus the answer is choice (E).

Remark for the advanced student: There is no reason that choice (E) has to be the answer. The values we got for x and y are not the only solutions to the given equations. x can also be -3, and y can also be approximately -2.236. If the answer we got didn't agree with any of the answer choices we would have to try other values for x and y (there are four possibilities all together).

A complete algebraic solution for the advanced student: I do **not** recommend solving the problem this way on the SAT.

There are two possibilities for x: x = 3 and x = -3

There are two possibilities for y: y = $\sqrt{5}$ and y = $-\sqrt{5}$

So, there are 4 possibilities for $(2x + y)^2$.

$(2*3 + \sqrt{5})^2 = (6 + \sqrt{5})(6 + \sqrt{5}) = 36 + 6\sqrt{5} + 6\sqrt{5} + 5 = 41 + 12\sqrt{5}$

Since this is answer choice (E) we can stop. We don't need to do the other three computations. The answer is choice (E).

106. The function g has the property that $g(a) = g(b)$ for all real numbers a and b. What is the graph of $y = g(x)$ in the xy-plane?

    (A) A parabola symmetric about the x-axis
    (B) A line with slope 0
    (C) A line with slope 1
    (D) A line with no slope
    (E) A semicircle centered at the origin

* The given property means that every number we substitute in for x gives the **same** value for y. Thus the graph is a horizontal line. A horizontal line has a slope of 0. Thus, the answer is choice (B).

107. Let * be defined by $x * y = x^y$. If $a = 3 * x$, $b = 3 * y$, and $x + y = 2$, what is the value of ab?

    (A) 1
    (B) 3
    (C) 9
    (D) 27
    (E) 81

Beginner Method: Let's choose values for x and y so that x + y = 2. Let's use x = 1 and y = 1. Then a = 3 * 1 = 3^1 = 3, and b = 3 * 1 = 3^1 = 3. Therefore ab = (3)(3) = 9, choice (C).

For more information on this technique, see **Strategy 4** in **"The 32 Most Effective SAT Math Strategies."**

* **Advanced Method:** a = 3*x = 3^x and b = 3*y = 3^y. It then follows that ab = $3^x 3^y = 3^{x+y} = 3^2$ = 9, choice (C).

See p. 57 of **"The 32 Most Effective SAT Math Strategies"** for a review of the basic laws of exponents.

108. Positive integers a, b, and c satisfy the equations $a^{-b} = \dfrac{1}{16}$ and $b^c = 256$. If $a < b$, what is the value of $a + b + c$?

    (A) 6
    (B) 8
    (C) 10
    (D) 14
    (E) 16

* 16 can be rewritten as 2^4, 4^2, or 16^1. So 1/16 can be written as 2^{-4}, 4^{-2}, or 16^{-1}. Since a < b, a = 2 and b = 4. When we raise 4 to the 4th power we get 256. Thus, c = 4, and a + b + c = 2 + 4 + 4 = 10, choice (C).

For a review of negative exponents see page 61 in **"The 32 Most Effective SAT Math Strategies."**

109. If x and y are each positive integers less than 12 and $\dfrac{x}{y}$ is equivalent to $\dfrac{3}{5}$, how many values of y are possible?

    (A) One
    (B) Two
    (C) Three
    (D) Four
    (E) Five

* A fraction is equivalent to 3/5 if it is equal to 3k/5k for some number k. We need only check integer values of k.

        k=1   3/5
        k=2   6/10
        k=3   9/15

15 is greater than 12 so we reject k=3. Thus we see there are two possibilities, choice (B).

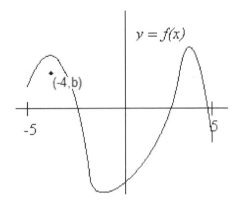

110. The figure above shows the graph of the function f and the point $(-4, b)$. For how many values of x between -5 and 5 does $f(x) = b$?

* We draw a horizontal line through the point (-4, b).

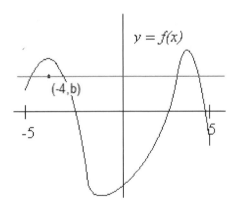

The horizontal line hits the graph 4 times. So f(x) = b for 4 values of x. Thus, the answer is **4**.

Remark: Each point on the horizontal line has the form (x, b), and each point on the curve has the form (x, f(x)). So, if a point is simultaneously on the horizontal line **and** the curve, f(x) = b.

111. For any real numbers r and s such that $r \neq s$, let $r \propto s$ be defined by $r \propto s = \dfrac{r+s}{r-s}$. If $r+s = 81$ and $r \propto s = 9$, what is the value of r?

* Substituting in the given values we get

9 = 81/(r − s), so that 9(r − s) = 81, and r − s = 9.

So we have the following simple system of equations.

$$r + s = 81$$
$$\underline{r - s = 9}$$
$$2r = 90$$

We got the last equation by adding the two prior equations. Finally, we divide both sides by 2 to get r = **45**.

112. For all numbers a and b, let $a \lozenge b = a^3 - 2ab$. What is the value of $(2 \lozenge 1) \lozenge 3$?

* Let's first compute 2 ◊ 1 = 2^3 − 2*2*1 = 8 − 4 = 4.

Now, (2 ◊ 1) ◊ 3 = 4 ◊ 3 = 4^3 − 2*4*3 = 64 − 24 = **40**.

103

LEVEL 4: GEOMETRY

113. Point A is a vertex of a 6-sided polygon. The polygon has 6 sides of equal length and 6 angles of equal measure. When all possible diagonals are drawn from point A in the polygon, how many triangles are formed?

   (A) One
   (B) Two
   (C) Three
   (D) Four
   (E) Six

* We draw a picture.

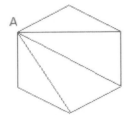

Observe that there are four triangles, choice (D).

For more information on this technique, see **Strategy 9** in **"The 32 Most Effective SAT Math Strategies."**

114. Points B, C, and D lie on a line in that order, and point A is not on the line. If $AB = AD$, which of the following must be true?

   (A) $AB > AC$
   (B) $AB > BC$
   (C) $AB > BD$
   (D) $AC > CD$
   (E) $BC > CD$

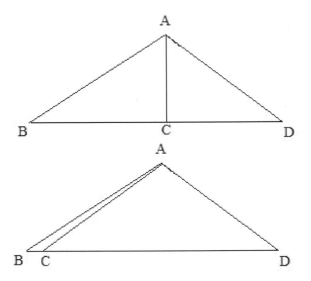

* The shortest distance from A to BD is the perpendicular distance as shown in the first figure above. As we move point C to the left or right along AD, the length of AC increases. In this way, we see that AB and AD will both be larger than AC as long as B < C < D. Therefore the answer is choice (A).

115. A container in the shape of a right circular cylinder has an inside base radius of 5 centimeters and an inside height of 6 centimeters. This cylinder is completely filled with fluid. All of the fluid is then poured into a second right circular cylinder with a larger inside base radius of 7 centimeters. What must be the minimum inside height, in centimeters, of the second container?

(A) $\dfrac{5}{\sqrt{7}}$

(B) $\dfrac{7}{5}$

(C) 5

(D) $\dfrac{150}{49}$

(E) $2\sqrt{7}$

* The volume of the first cylinder is V = $\pi r^2 h$ = $\pi(5^2)(6)$ = 150π. The volume of the second cylinder is V = $\pi r^2 h$ = $\pi(7^2)h$ = 49hπ. We set the two volumes equal to each other and solve for h.

$$150\pi = 49h\pi$$
$$h = 150/49, \text{ choice (D)}.$$

Remark: The formula for the volume of a right circular cylinder is given at the beginning of each math section on the SAT.

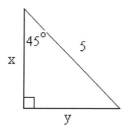

116. In the triangle above, what is the value of $x + y$?

    (A) 1

    (B) $\dfrac{5\sqrt{2}}{2}$ (approximately 3.54)

    (C) 5

    (D) $5\sqrt{2}$ (approximately 7.07)

    (E) 10

Solution using special triangles: Note that this is a 45, 45, 90 right triangle. Using the special triangle given at the beginning of each math section of the SAT we see that x and y are both equal to s, and $s\sqrt{2}$ = 5. Therefore

$$x + y = s + s = 5/\sqrt{2} + 5/\sqrt{2} \sim 7.07.$$

Thus, the answer is choice (D).

Remark: Without using a calculator we see that

106

$$x + y = 10/\sqrt{2} = (10\sqrt{2})/2 = 5\sqrt{2}.$$

Note that we get from the second to the third step above by **rationalizing** the denominator. That is, we multiply the numerator and denominator of $10/\sqrt{2}$ by $\sqrt{2}$ to get $(10/\sqrt{2})(\sqrt{2}/\sqrt{2}) = (10\sqrt{2})/2$.

As you can see it is much easier to just use the calculator.

For more information on this technique, see **Strategy 27** in **"The 32 Most Effective SAT Math Strategies."**

Solution using the Pythagorean Theorem: Since two of the angles have equal measure (they both measure 45 degrees), the triangle is isosceles, and we see that x = y. By the Pythagorean Theorem

$$x^2 + x^2 = 5^2$$
$$2x^2 = 25$$
$$x^2 = 25/2$$
$$x = 5/\sqrt{2}$$

Therefore $x + y = x + x = 5/\sqrt{2} + 5/\sqrt{2} \sim 7.07$, choice (D).

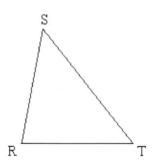

Note: Figure not drawn to scale.

117. In the triangle above, $RS = RT = 13$ and $ST = 10$. What is the area of the triangle?

* We choose ST as the base, and draw altitude RP from vertex R to base ST.

107

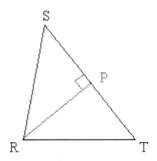

Note: Figure not drawn to scale.

In an isosceles triangle the altitude is equal to the median. It follows that TP =1/2 ST = 5. Using the Pythagorean triple 5, 12, 13, we have RP = 12.

Area = 1/2 bh = 1/2 (10)(12) = **60**.

Remarks:

(1) An **altitude** of a triangle is perpendicular to the base. A **median** of a triangle splits the base into two equal parts. In an isosceles triangle, the altitude and median are equal (when you choose the base that is **not** one of the equal sides).

(2) We chose ST to be the base because it is the side that is not one of the equal sides.

(3) 3, 4, 5 and 5, 12, 13 are the two most common Pythagorean triples. These sets of numbers satisfy the Pythagorean theorem.

(4) If you don't remember the Pythagorean triples it is no big deal. Just use the Pythagorean theorem. In this case,

$$5^2 + b^2 = 13^2$$
$$25 + b^2 = 169$$
$$b^2 = 169 - 25 = 144$$
$$b = 12.$$

118. Points P and Q are on the surface of a sphere that has a volume of 288π cubic meters. What is the greatest possible length, in meters, of line segment PQ? (The volume of a sphere with radius r is $V = \dfrac{4}{3}\pi r^3$.)

* PQ will be greatest when it is a diameter of the sphere.

We are given that 4/3 πr^3 = 288π. Thus r^3 = 288*3/4 = 216, and r = 6. So the radius of the sphere is 6, and therefore the diameter of the sphere is 2*6 = **12**.

119. In the xy-plane, line ℓ is the graph of $3x + ky = 7$, where k is a constant. The graph of $6x + 16y = 11$ is parallel to line ℓ. What is the value of k?

* Since we multiply 3 by 2 to get 6, we multiply k by 2 to get 16. Therefore k = **8**.

Remark: The equations ax + by = e and cx + dy = f have graphs that are parallel lines if there is a number h such that ha = c and hb = d. In the given problem, h = 2.

Note that if he = f also, then the two equations represent the same line. In the given problem this is **not** the case. Therefore the lines are distinct (but parallel).

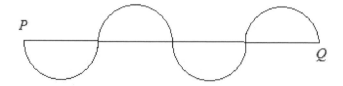

120. In the figure above, the diameters of the four semicircles are equal and lie on line segment PQ. If the length of line segment PQ is $\dfrac{48}{\pi}$, what is the length of the curve from P to Q?

109

* The diameter of each semicircle is 48/π ÷ 4 = 12/π. Thus the circumference of each semicircle is 1/2 * π * 12/π = 6. Since we are adding up the lengths of four such semicircles, the answer is 4*6 = **24**.

Remark: The circumference of a circle with radius r is C = 2πr (or C = πd where d is the diameter of the circle). This formula is given on the SAT. Since a semicircle is half of a circle, the circumference of a semicircle with radius r is C = πr (or C = πd/2).

LEVEL 4: PROBABILITY AND STATISTICS

121. If the average (arithmetic mean) of a, b, and 17 is 11, what is the average of a and b ?

   (A) $5\dfrac{1}{3}$
   (B) 8
   (C) 9
   (D) 16
   (E) It cannot be determined from the information given.

* We change the average to a sum using the formula

Sum = Average * Number

So the Sum of the 3 numbers is 11*3 = 33.

Thus a + b + 17 = 33, and it follows that a + b = 16.

We now use the above formula again in the form

Average = Sum/Number

So the average of the 2 numbers is 16/2 = 8, choice (B).

For more information on this technique, see **Strategy 20** in **"The 32 Most Effective SAT Math Strategies."**

Solution by picking numbers: Let's let a = 5 and b = 11. We make this choice because 5 and 17 are both 6 units from 11. Then the average of a and b is (a + b)/2 = (5 + 11)/2 = 16/2 = 8, choice (B).

For more information on this technique, see **Strategy 4** in **"The 32 Most Effective SAT Math Strategies."**

Remark: Even though we never ruled out choice (E) as the answer, Quasi-elimination says that we are probably correct. See **Strategy 10** in **"The 32 Most Effective SAT Math Strategies"** for more information.

122. Twenty one people were playing a game. 1 person scored 50 points, 2 people scored 60 points, 3 people scored 70 points, 4 people scored 80 points, 5 people scored 90 points, and 6 people scored 100 points. Which of the following correctly shows the order of the median, mode and average (arithmetic mean) of the 21 scores?

   (A) average < median< mode
   (B) average < mode < median
   (C) median < mode < average
   (D) median < average < mode
   (E) mode < median < average

* The median of 21 numbers is the 11th number when the numbers are listed in increasing order.

$$50, 60, 60, 70, 70, 70, 80, 80, 80, 80, \mathbf{90}.$$

So we see that the median is 90.

The mode is the number that appears most frequently. This is clearly **100**.

Finally, we compute the average.

$(1*50 + 2*60 + 3*70 + 4*80 + 5*90 + 6*100)/21 = 1750/21 \sim 83.33.$

Thus, we see that average < median < mode. This is choice (A).

123. The average (arithmetic mean) of 4 numbers is x. If one of the numbers is y, what is the average of the remaining 3 numbers in terms of x and y?

(A) $\dfrac{x}{4}$

(B) $4x - y$

(C) $\dfrac{3x - y}{4}$

(D) $\dfrac{4x - y}{3}$

(E) $\dfrac{4y - x}{3}$

Beginner Method: We will use the technique of **picking numbers**. Let's let y = 5, and we'll let the other 3 numbers be 1, 2, and 4. We then have that x = (1 + 2 + 4 + 5)/4 = 12/4 = 3, and the average of the remaining 3 numbers is (1 + 2 + 4)/3 = 7/3 ~ **2.333**. We now substitute x = 3 and y = 5 into all five answer choices.

(A) 3/4 = .75
(B) 4*3 − 5 = 12 − 5 = 7
(C) (3*3 − 5)/4 = (9 − 5)/4 = 4/4 = 1
(D) (4*3 − 5)/3 = (12 − 5)/3 = 7/3 ~ 2.333
(E) (4*5 − 3)/3 = (20 − 3)/3 = 17/3 ~5.667

Since (A), (B), (C) and (E) are incorrect we can eliminate them. Therefore the answer is choice (D).

For more information on this technique, see **Strategy 4** in **"The 32 Most Effective SAT Math Strategies."**

* Advanced Method: We use the formula

Sum = Average * Number

So the Sum of the 4 numbers is 4x.

The sum of the remaining 3 numbers (after removing y) is 4x − y.

We now use the above formula again in the form

Average = Sum/Number

So the Average of the remaining 3 numbers is (4x − y)/3, choice (D).

For more information on this technique, see **Strategy 20** in **"The 32 Most Effective SAT Math Strategies."**

124. The average (arithmetic mean) of x, $2x$, y, and $4y$ is $2x$, what is y in terms of x ?

(A) $\dfrac{x}{4}$

(B) $\dfrac{x}{2}$

(C) x

(D) $\dfrac{3x}{2}$

(E) $2x$

* We use the formula

Sum = Average * Number

So x + 2x + y + 4y = (2x)(4). That is 3x + 5y = 8x. Subtracting 3x from both sides of this equation yields 5y = 5x. Finally, we divide each side of this last equation by 5 to get y = x, choice (C).

For more information on this technique, see **Strategy 20** in **"The 32 Most Effective SAT Math Strategies."**

125. If the average (arithmetic mean) of the measures of two noncongruent angles of an isosceles triangle is 80°, which of the following is the measure of one of the angles of the triangle?

    (A) 110°
    (B) 120°
    (C) 130°
    (D) 140°
    (E) 150°

* We change the average to a sum using the formula

Sum = Average * Number

So the Sum of the measures of the two noncongruent angles of the isosceles triangle is 80*2 = 160°.

Thus, the third angle is 180 − 160 = 20°. Since the triangle is isosceles, one of the original angles must also be 20°. It follows that the other original angle was 180 − 20 − 20 = 140°, choice (D).

Note: At first glance it seems that there might be another possibility. If the third angle has measure 20°, then the other two could each have measure 80°. But this would contradict that the original two angles are noncongruent!

For more information on this technique, see **Strategy 20** in **"The 32 Most Effective SAT Math Strategies."**

126. A wall is to be painted one color with a stripe of a different color running through the middle. If 7 different colors are available, how many color combinations are possible?

* **Solution using the counting principle:** The counting principle says that when you perform events in succession you multiply the number of possibilities. There are 7 ways to choose a color for the wall. Once this color is chosen there are now 6 ways to choose a color for the stripe. Thus, there are 7*6 = **42** possibilities.

Solution by making a list: Let's assume the colors are red, blue, green, yellow, purple, orange, and white. We will list all the possibilities in a nice way:

RB, RG, RY, RP, RO, RW
BR, BG, BY, BP, BO, BW
GR, GB, GY, GP, GO, GW
YR, YB, YG, YP, YO, YW
PR, PB, PG, PY, PO, PW
OR, OB, OG, OY, OP, OW
WR, WB, WG, WY, WP, WO

In the above list, we abbreviated each color by using the first letter of its name. The first position is for the wall, and the second for the stripe. We see that we have listed **42** possibilities.

Remark: I don't recommend solving the problem this way on the SAT. However, while practicing SAT problems it is a good idea to write out these lists until you have a good understanding of why the counting principle works.

For more information on this technique, see **Strategy 21** in **"The 32 Most Effective SAT Math Strategies."**

A more sophisticated solution without listing: We can use a permutation. There are $_7P_6$ = 7*6 = **42** ways to choose 2 colors from 6, and place them in a specific order.

Important note: Don't let the word "combinations" in the problem itself trick you. This is **not** a combination in the mathematical sense. If you paint the wall red and the stripe blue, then this is a **different** choice from painting the wall blue and the stripe red.

See the solution to problem 63 in this book for a more detailed explanation of permutations.

127. A pet store has a white dog, a black dog, and a grey dog. The store also has three cats – one white, one black, and one grey – and three birds – one white, one black, and one grey. Jonathon wants to buy one dog, one cat, and one bird. He wants one to be white, one black, and one grey. How many different possibilities does he have?

* Solution using the counting principle: The counting principle says that when you perform events in succession you multiply the number of possibilities. There are 3 ways to choose a dog. Once the dog is chosen there are now 2 ways to choose a cat. Finally, after choosing a dog and cat, there is 1 way to choose a bird. Thus, there are 3*2*1 = **6** possibilities.

Solution by making a list: Let's list all the possibilities in a nice way:

WBG   WGB   BWG   BGW   GWB   GBW

In the above list, W stands for white, B for black, and G for grey. The first position is for the dog, the second for the cat, and the third for the bird. We see that there are **6** possibilities.

For more information on this technique, see **Strategy 21** in **"The 32 Most Effective SAT Math Strategies."**

A more sophisticated solution without listing: We can use a permutation. There are $_3P_3 = 3! = 1*2*3 = $ **6** ways to arrange 3 colors.

See the solution to problem 63 in this book for a more detailed explanation of permutations.

128. Any 2 points determine a line. If there are 8 points in a plane, no 3 of which lie on the same line, how many lines are determined by pairs of these 8 points?

* We need to count the number of ways to choose 2 points from 8. This is the combination $_8C_2 = $ **28**.

116

Combinations: $_8C_2$ means the number of **combinations** of 8 things taken 2 at a time. In a combination order does not matter (as opposed to the **permutation** $_8P_2$ where the order does matter).

$$_8P_2 = 8!/6! = 8*7 = 56$$
$$_8C_2 = 8!/[6!2!] = 8*7/2 = 56/2 = 28$$

In general, if n is an integer, then n! = 1*2*3*...*n
If n and k are integers, then $_nP_r = n!/(n-r)!$ and $_nC_r = n!/[r!(n-r)!]$

On the SAT you do **not** need to know these formulas. You can do these computations very quickly on your graphing calculator. For example, to compute $_8C_2$, type 8 into your calculator, then in the **Math** menu scroll over to **Prb** and select **nCr** (or press **3**). Then type 2 and hit **Enter**. You will get an answer of **28**.

LEVEL 5: NUMBER THEORY

129. In an empty square field, *n* rows of *n* trees are planted so that the whole field is filled with trees. If *k* of these trees lie along the boundary of the field, which of the following is a possible value for *k* ?

    (A) 14
    (B) 49
    (C) 86
    (D) 125
    (E) 276

* We will systematically try values for n, and draw a picture of the situation to determine the corresponding value for k.

Here is the picture for n = 3.

Note that k = 9 − 1 = 8.

Here is the picture for n = 4.

Note that k = 16 − 4 = 12.

Here is the picture for n = 5.

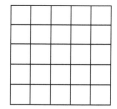

Note that k = 25 − 9 = 16.

So the pattern appears to be 8, 12, 16, 20, 24, 28,…
Make sure that you keep drawing pictures until this is clear to you.
So we see that the answer must be divisible by 4.

Beginning with choice (C) we have 86/4 = 21.5. So choice (C) is not the answer.

We can eliminate choices (B) and (D) because they end in an odd digit. Trying choice (E) we have 276/4 = 69. Thus 276 is divisible by 4, and choice (E) is the answer.

For more information on this technique, see **Strategy 17** in **"The 32 Most Effective SAT Math Strategies."** Also relevant to this problem are **Strategies 1 and 9**.

For the advanced student: Let's prove that for each n, the corresponding k is divisible by 4.

For fixed n, the total number of trees is n^2, and the number of trees **not** on the boundary is $(n-2)^2 = n^2 - 4n + 4$. Thus, the number of trees on the boundary is

$$k = n^2 - (n^2 - 4n + 4) = n^2 - n^2 + 4n - 4 = 4n - 4 = 4(n-1)$$

which is divisible by 4.

130. If x and y are integers and $x^2 y + xy^2 + x^2 y^2$ is odd, which of the following statements must be true?

> I. x is odd
> II. xy is odd
> III. $x + y + xy$ is odd

    (A) I only
    (B) II only
    (C) III only
    (D) I and III only
    (E) I, II, and III

* Note that $x^2y + xy^2 = xy(x + y + xy)$. The only way a product can be odd is if each factor is odd. Therefore x, y and x + y + xy all must be odd. Since the product of two odd integers is odd, xy must also be odd. So the answer is choice (E).

131. If $a^6 b^5 c^4 d^3 > 0$, which of the following products must be positive?

    (A) ab
    (B) ac
    (C) bc
    (D) ad
    (E) bd

Beginner Method: Let's plug in numbers for a, b, c, and d that make the given expression positive. Let's try a = 1, b = -1, c = -1, d = -1. Then $a^6b^5c^4d^3 = (1)(-1)(1)(-1) = 1 > 0$. So the given condition is satisfied. Now let's check the answer choices.

(A) $(1)(-1) = -1$

(B) $(1)(-1) = -1$

(C) $(-1)(-1) = 1$

(D) $(1)(-1) = -1$

(E) $(-1)(-1) = 1$

So we can eliminate choices (A), (B), and (D). Let's try another set of numbers, say a = 1, b = 1, c = -1, d = 1. In this case we now have $a^6b^5c^4d^3 = (1)(1)(1)(1) = 1 > 0$. Let's check the remaining answer choices.

(C) $(1)(-1) = -1$

(E) $(1)(1) = 1$

So we can eliminate choice (C), and the answer is choice (E).

For more information on this technique, see **Strategy 4** in **"The 32 Most Effective SAT Math Strategies."**

* Advanced Method: In order for the given product to be positive, b and d must have the same sign. Therefore bd must be positive, choice (E).

Remark: The advanced solution depends on the fact that when you raise a negative number to an even power you get a positive number, and when you raise a negative number to an odd power you get a negative number.

132. If $\dfrac{st}{u}$ is an integer which of the following must also be an integer?

    (A) stu

    (B) $\dfrac{3s^2t^2}{u^2}$

    (C) $\dfrac{su}{t}$

    (D) $\dfrac{tu}{s}$

    (E) $\dfrac{s}{tu}$

Beginner Method: Let's pick numbers for s, t, and u. Let's try s = 3, t = 4, and u = 2. Then st/u = 3*4/2 = 6, an integer. So the given condition is satisfied. Now let's check the answer choices.

    (A) 3*4*2 = 24

    (B) 3(9)(16)/4 = 108

    (C) 3*2/4 = 1.5

    (D) 4*2/3 ~ 2.67

    (E) 3/(4*2) = .375

So we can eliminate choices (C), (D), and (E). Let's try another set of numbers, say s = .5, t = 1, and u = .5. Then st/u = .5*1/.5 = 1, an integer. Let's check the remaining answer choices.

    (A) .5*1*.5 = .25

    (B) 3(.25)(1)/.25 = 3

So we can eliminate choice (A), and the answer is choice (B).

* Advanced Method: Let st/u be an integer. Then $3s^2t^2/u^2 = 3(st/u)^2$ is an integer because the product of integers is an integer.

121

Remark: If you are having trouble seeing that the expression in the advanced method is an integer, the following might help. Since st/u is an integer, we can write st/u = k for some integer k. It follows that

$$3s^2t^2/u^2 = 3(st/u)^2 = 3k^2.$$

Note that $3k^2$ is an integer because the set of integers is closed under multiplication.

Quasi-elimination note: Choice (A) almost seems like an obvious answer because it has no denominator. Since this is a Level 5 problem we can quasi-eliminate this choice. See **Strategy 10** in **"The 32 Most Effective SAT Math Strategies"** for more information.

⚡ 133. If n is a positive integer and $k = n^3 - n$, which of the following statements about k must be true for all values of n?

> I. k is a multiple of 3
> II. k is a multiple of 4
> III. k is a multiple of 6

    (A) I only
    (B) II only
    (C) III only
    (D) I and III only
    (E) I, II, and III

Beginner Method: Let's try some values for n.

n = 2. Then k = 6. This shows that II can be false. So we can eliminate choices (B) and (E).

n = 3. Then k = 24. This is divisible by both 3 and 6.

n = 4. Then k = 60. This is again divisible by both 3 and 6.

The evidence seems to suggest that the answer is choice (D).

Remark: This method is a bit risky. Since this is a Level 5 problem, there is a chance that some large value of n might provide a counterexample. In this case, it turns out not to be the case, and the answer is in fact choice (D).

* Advanced Method: $n^3 - n = n(n^2 - 1) = n(n - 1)(n + 1) = (n - 1)n(n + 1)$.

Thus $n^3 - n$ is a product of 3 consecutive integers. In a product of 2 consecutive integers, one of the integers must be divisible by 2 (even). In a product of 3 consecutive integers, one of the integers must be divisible by 3. Therefore $n^3 - n$ is divisible by both 2 and 3, and thus it is divisible by 6. As in the beginner method above, n = 2 shows that the expression does **not** have to be divisible by 4. Thus, the answer is choice (D).

Exercise for the very advanced student: Let k be any positive integer. Show that the product of k consecutive integers is divisible by k!

134. How many positive integers less than 5,000 are multiples of 7 and are equal to 11 times an even integer?

* Note that 11 times an even integer is just a multiple of 11*2 = 22. So we are looking for positive integers less than 5,000 that are multiples of both 7 and 22. Since 7 and 22 have no prime factors in common, we are just looking for multiples of 7*22 = 154 that are less than 5000. The answer is just the integer part of 5000/154 ~ 32.4675. So we grid in **32**.

135. In how many of the integers from 1 to 150 does the digit 6 appear at least once?

* Let's list these integers **carefully**.

6, 16, 26, 36, 46, 56, **60, 61, 62, 63, 64, 65, 66, 67, 68, 69,** 76, 86, 96, 106, 116, 126, 136, 146

We see that there are **24** such integers.

For more information on this technique, see **Strategy 21** in **"The 32 Most Effective SAT Math Strategies."**

Solution using the counting principle: We start by finding the number of integers that **do not** contain a 6. There are two cases to consider:

(Case 1) The number is of the form abc where a = 1 and b < 5: In this case there are 5 possibilities for b (the second digit), and 9 possibilities for c (the third digit – note that this digit can be anything but 6). Thus there are 5*9 = 45 possibilities.

(Case 2) The number is of the form abc where a = 0: In this case there are 9 possibilities for b (the second digit), and 9 possibilities for c (the third digit). Thus there are 9*9 = 81 possibilities.

So there are 45 + 81 = 126 possibilities that **do not** contain a 6. Therefore there are 150 − 126 = **24** possibilities that contain a 6.

Remarks:

(1) Usually, you don't let the lead digits be zero, but this time we want to count one digit numbers and two digit numbers as well -- this method includes them in the count.

(2) In Case 2 we included the "number" 000, but that's okay because we excluded 150 from Case 1. So the total is correct.

(3) The method of listing is much easier in this problem.

136. If n is a positive integer such that the units (ones) digit of $n^2 + 4n$ is 7 and the units digit of n is <u>not</u> 7, what is the units digit of $n + 3$?

* By plugging in values of n, we find that for n = 9,

$$n^2 + 4n = 9^2 + 4*9 = 81 + 36 = 117.$$

So n = 9 works, and n + 3 = 9 + 3 = 12. So the units digit of n + 3 is **2**.

Advanced solution showing the independence of n: $n^2 + 4n = n(n + 4)$. So we are looking at positive integers 4 units apart whose product ends in 7. Since 7 is odd, n must be odd. So n must end in 1, 3, 5, or 9. Note that we skip n = 7 since the problem forbids us from using it.

If n ends in 1, then n + 4 ends in 5, and n(n + 4) ends in 5.
If n ends in 3, then n + 4 ends in 7, and n(n + 4) ends in 1.
If n ends in 5, then n + 4 ends in 9, and n(n + 4) ends in 5.
If n ends in 9, then n + 4 ends in 13, and n(n + 4) ends in **7**.

So n ends in a 9, and n + 3 ends in a **2**.

LEVEL 5: ALGEBRA AND FUNCTIONS

137. For how many integers n is $(5n - 29)(3n + 7)$ a negative number?

 (A) None
 (B) Two
 (C) Four
 (D) Six
 (E) Eight

* We first figure out the **real** numbers where the expression is 0. To do this just set each factor to 0:

$5n - 29 = 0$ $3n + 7 = 0$
     $5n = 29$ $3n = -7$
       $n = 29/5 = 5.8$ $n = -7/3 \sim -2.333$

We want to find all integer solutions of the inequality

$$(5n - 29)(3n + 7) < 0.$$

A good guess is to just count all the integers between -2.333 and 5.8. We have -2, -1, 0, 1, 2, 3, 4, and 5. Thus it seems that there are **eight** (more explanation below the remark). The answer to this question is in fact choice (E).

Remark: We choose the "inside" of the two numbers because the answer choices indicate that there must be finitely many solutions - the "outsides" give infinitely many solutions.

Deeper understanding of the mathematics: The given expression is a polynomial (in particular, it is quadratic, so that its graph is a parabola). Polynomials are "continuous everywhere," that is you never lift your pencil from your paper when drawing them. Thus, the only way they can change from positive to negative (or vice versa) is by passing through zero. So once you find the zeros, you need only test one value in each of the intervals determined by these zeros (in this case there are three) to determine if you get negative or positive results in the **whole** interval.

Thus, we need only test 3 values to be certain of our answer - one value less than -2.333, one value between -2.333 and 5.8, and one value greater than 5.8. I will choose the numbers -3, 0, and 6:

$n = -3$: $(5n - 29)(3n + 7) = (5(-3) - 29)(3(-3) + 7) = (-44)(-2) > 0$.

$n = 0$: $(5n - 29)(3n + 7) = (5(0) - 29)(3(0) + 7) = (-29)(7) < 0$.

$n = 6$: $(5n - 29)(3n + 7) = (5(6) - 29)(3(6) + 7) = (1)(25) > 0$.

Notice that we didn't need to finish these computations to determine if the result was positive or negative. We just used the fact that the product of 2 negatives is positive, the product of a negative and a positive is negative, and the product of two positives is positive.

Since 0 gave a negative answer, any number in the interval from 2.333 to 5.8 will give a negative answer. Similarly, any number less than 2.333 will give a positive answer, as will any number greater than 5.8.

We have now verified that choice (E) is the answer.

Graphical Analysis: The graph of $f(n) = (5n - 29)(3n + 7)$ is an upward facing parabola. To see this we can FOIL the expression to get

$$f(n) = 15n^2 - 52n - 203.$$

All we actually need here is that the first term is $15n^2$. Since 15 is positive, the parabola faces upwards. This analysis shows that it is the middle portion which is negative. So we need only count the integers between -2.333 and 5.8. This can be verified by graphing the function in your graphing calculator.

Alternatively, if either of the external intervals were negative, then there would be an infinite number of integer solutions. Since there is no answer choice that allows for this possibility, the only reasonable place to look is between the given roots.

$$x = 16z$$
$$y = 16z^2 + 2$$

138. If $z > 0$ in the equation above, what is y in terms of x ?

(A) $\dfrac{1}{16}x^2 + 1$

(B) $\dfrac{1}{16}x^2 + 2$

(C) $\dfrac{1}{16}x^2 + 16$

(D) $\dfrac{1}{4}x^2 + 2$

(E) $x^2 + 16$

Solution by picking numbers: Let's choose a value for z, say z = 1. It follows that x = 16 and y = 18. Let's substitute x = 16 into each answer choice:

(A) 17
(B) 18
(C) 32
(D) 66
(E) 272

Since (A), (C), (D) and (E) are incorrect we can eliminate them. Therefore the answer is choice (B).

Important note: (B) is **not** the correct answer simply because it is equal to 18. It is correct because all 4 of the other choices are **not** 18.

For more information on this technique, see **Strategy 4** in **"The 32 Most Effective SAT Math Strategies."**

* An algebraic solution: We first solve for z in the first equation:

$$z = x/16$$

Now substitute this into the second equation:

$y = 16z^2 + 2 = 16(x/16)^2 + 2 = 16x^2/(16)^2 + 2 = x^2/16 + 2$. This is the same as choice (B).

139. If a and b are positive integers, which of the following is equivalent to $(3a)^{5b} - (3a)^{2b}$?

(A) $(3a)^{3b}$

(B) $3^b(a^5 - a^2)$

(C) $(3a)^{2b}[(3a)^{3b} - 1]$

(D) $(3a)^{2b}[9a^b - 1]$

(E) $(3a)^{2b}[(3a)^5 - 1]$

Beginner Method: Let's pick some numbers for a and b, say a = b = 1. Then $(3a)^{5b} - (3a)^{2b} = 3^5 - 3^2 =$ **234**. Put a nice big, dark circle around this number. Let's substitute a = b = 1 into each answer choice.

(A) $3^3 = 27$

(B) $3(1 - 1) = 0$

(C) $3^2[3^3 - 1] = 234$

(D) $3^2[9 - 1] = 72$

(E) $3^2[3^5 - 1] = 2178$

Since (A), (B), (D), and (E) all came out incorrect, the answer is choice (C).

Remark: In "The 32 Most Effective SAT Math Strategies" I had stated that it is usually best to avoid numbers that are too simple such as 1. I also stated that it is best to pick different numbers for different variables. I have violated these guidelines here, because I see that the exponents can make the numbers get quite large very fast if I were to plug in larger numbers. In this particular case violating these guidelines worked out to our advantage.

For more information on this technique, see **Strategy 4** in **"The 32 Most Effective SAT Math Strategies."**

Advanced Method: Let's consider 3a as a block, and rename it x. So $(3a)^{5b} - (3a)^{2b} = x^{5b} - x^{2b} = x^{2b}(x^{3b} - 1) = (3a)^{2b}[(3a)^{3b} - 1]$, choice (C).

For more information on this technique, see **Strategy 19** in **"The 32 Most Effective SAT Math Strategies."**

Remark: In going from step 2 to step 3 in the sequence of equations above, we factored, and used the following rule of exponents.

$$x^z x^w = x^{z+w}$$

If you are having trouble seeing this, look at the equation in reverse:

$$x^{2b}(x^{3b} - 1) = x^{2b}x^{3b} - x^{2b} = x^{2b+3b} - x^{2b} = x^{5b} - x^{2b}$$

Also note that we don't actually need to perform a substitution here. We can solve this problem in one step as follows.

$$(3a)^{5b} - (3a)^{2b} = (3a)^{2b}[(3a)^{3b} - 1].$$

For a review of the laws of exponents, see page 57 in **"The 32 Most Effective SAT Math Strategies."**

$$k = a - b + 16$$
$$k = b - c - 7$$
$$k = c - d - 9$$
$$k = d - a + 12$$

140. In the system of equations above, what is the value of k ?

    (A) 1
    (B) 2
    (C) 3
    (D) 4
    (E) 5

* Notice that when we add the four given equations, all the variables on the right hand side add to zero. So 4k = 16 − 7 − 9 + 12 = 12. Therefore k = 12/4 = 3, choice (C).

For more information on this technique, see **Strategy 16** in **"The 32 Most Effective SAT Math Strategies."**

141. If $x^2 + y^2 = k^2$, and $xy = 8 - 4k$, what is $(x + y)^2$ in terms of k ?

    (A) $k - 4$
    (B) $(k - 4)^2$
    (C) $k^2 - 4k + 8$
    (D) $(k - 2)^2 + 4$
    (E) $(k + 4)^2$

* $(x + y)^2 = (x + y)(x + y) = x^2 + 2xy + y^2 = x^2 + y^2 + 2xy = k^2 + 2(8 - 4k)$

    $= k^2 + 16 - 8k = k^2 - 8k + 16 = (k - 4)^2$, choice (B).

x	-2	-1	0	1
y	7	a	b	c

142. The values of x and y in the table above are related so that $(y-2)$ is directly proportional to $(x+3)$. What is the value of $a+b-c$?

* Beginning with the first column we see that y − 2 = 5 and x + 3 = 1. So the constant of proportionality is 5 (because 5*1 = 5). Thus, for each of the other columns we multiply (x + 3) by 5 to get (y − 2).

So we have,

$$5(-1 + 3) = a - 2, \text{ or equivalently, } a = 12$$
$$5(0 + 3) = b - 2, \text{ or equivalently, } b = 17$$
$$5(1 + 3) = c - 2, \text{ or equivalently, } c = 22$$

Thus, a + b − c = 12 + 17 − 22 = **7**.

A more formal algebraic solution:

y -2 = k(x + 3) for some constant k. To find k we use the first column:

$$7 - 2 = k(-2 + 3), \text{ or } 5 = k.$$

Thus,

$$y - 2 = 5(x + 3), \text{ or equivalently } y = 5x + 17$$

So,

$$\text{when } x = -1, a = 5(-1) + 17 = 12$$
$$\text{when } x = 0, b = 5(0) + 17 = 17$$
$$\text{when } x = 1, c = 5(1) + 17 = 22.$$

As before, a + b − c = 12 + 17 − 22 = **7**.

Definition: y is directly proportional to x if y = kx for some constant k.

143. Let g be a function such that $g(x) = k(x-5)(x+5)$ where k is a nonzero constant. If $g(b-3.7) = 0$ and $b > 0$, what is the value of b?

* From the form of g we see that g(5) = 0. So let's try b − 3.7 = 5. It follows that b = 5 + 3.7 = **8.7**.

Remark: It is also true that g(-5) = 0. But setting b − 3.7 = -5 gives us that b = -5 + 3.7 = -1.3, a negative number. The given condition of b > 0 means that we must reject this solution. Also, we cannot grid in a negative answer on the SAT.

$$(x - n)(x - 9) = x^2 - 4nx + k$$

144. In the equation above, n and k are constants. If the equation is true for all values of x, what is the value of k?

Beginner Method: Let's plug in some simple values for x.

x = 0: 9n = k

x = 9: 0 = 81 − 36n + k

Substituting 9n for k in the second equation yields 0 = 81 − 27n, so that 27n = 81, and n = 81/27 = 3. Finally, k = 9n = 9*3 = **27**.

Intermediate Method: Multiply out the left hand side (FOIL) to get

$$x^2 - 9x - nx + 9n = x^2 - (9 + n)x + 9n$$

Setting the coefficient of x on the left equal to the coefficient of x on the right yields -(9 + n) = -4n, or 9 + n = 4n, or 3n = 9. So n = 3. Equating the constant terms on left and right yields 9n = k. Substituting 3 in for n gives k = 9*3 = **27**.

* **Advanced Method:** The left hand side is 0 when x = 9 and x = n. The coefficient of x is the negative of the sum of these roots, so 4n = n + 9, or 3n = 9. So n = 3. The constant term is the product of these roots, so that k = 9*3 = **27**.

Remark: In the advanced solution we have used the following fact about quadratic equations:

Let r and s be the roots of the quadratic equation $x^2 + bx + c = 0$. Then

$b = -(r + s)$ and $c = rs$.

Note: With a little practice, the advanced method can be done in your head in less than 10 seconds.

LEVEL 5: GEOMETRY

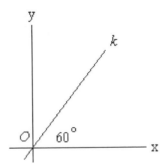

145. In the figure above, what is the equation of line k ?

(A) $y = \dfrac{x}{2}$

(B) $y = \dfrac{x}{\sqrt{2}}$

(C) $y = \dfrac{x}{\sqrt{3}}$

(D) $y = \sqrt{2}x$

(E) $y = \sqrt{3}x$

* We begin by forming a 30, 60, 90 triangle. If we let x = 1 in the special triangle given to us at the beginning of each math section of the SAT we get the following picture.

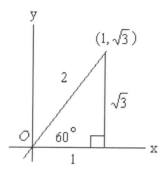

Note that we plotted the point by going right 1, then up $\sqrt{3}$. The slope of the line is m = $\sqrt{3}$ /1 = $\sqrt{3}$. Since the line passes through the origin, we have b = 0. Thus the equation of the line in slope-intercept form is

y = mx + b = $\sqrt{3}$ x + 0. So y = $\sqrt{3}$ x, choice (E).

For more information on this technique, see **Strategies 27** and **28** in **"The 32 Most Effective SAT Math Strategies."**

146. The lengths of the sides of an isosceles triangle are 16, n, and n. If n is an integer, what is the smallest possible perimeter of the triangle?

    (A) 30
    (B) 31
    (C) 32
    (D) 34
    (E) 48

We use the **triangle rule** which says that the third side of a triangle is between the sum and difference of the other two sides. So we have that n - n < 16 < n + n. That is, 0 < 16 < 2n. So n > 16/2 = 8. Therefore the smallest integer that n can be is n = 9, and it follows that the perimeter of the triangle is 16 + 9 + 9 = 34, choice (D).

* A slightly quicker solution: For this particular question we actually only need that the third side of the triangle is less than the sum of the other two sides. So we have that 16 < n + n = 2n, and so n > 16/2 = 8. Once again, it follows that we should let n = 9, and thus the perimeter is 16 + 9 + 9 = 34, choice (D).

For more information on this technique, see **Strategy 25** in **"The 32 Most Effective SAT Math Strategies.**

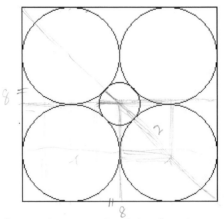

147. In the figure above, each of the four large circles is tangent to two of the other large circles, the small circle, and two sides of the square. If the diameter of each of the large circles is 4, what is the <u>radius</u> of the small circle?

    (A) $\sqrt{2}$ (approximately 1.414)
    (B)   1
    (C) $2\sqrt{2} - 2$ (approximately 0.828)
    (D) $\dfrac{1}{2}$
    (E) $\sqrt{2} - 1$ (approximately 0.414)

* We draw an isosceles right triangle.

135

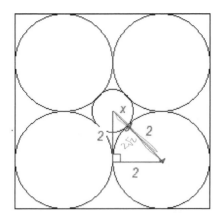

Note that each length labeled with a 2 is equal to the radius of one of the larger circles (the radius is half the diameter). The length labeled x is the radius of the smaller circle. An isosceles right triangle is the same as a 45, 45, 90 right triangle. By looking at the formula for this special triangle (given on the SAT) we see that $x + 2 = 2\sqrt{2}$ and so $x = 2\sqrt{2} - 2$, choice (C).

For more information on this technique, see **Strategy 27** in **"The 32 Most Effective SAT Math Strategies."**

Remark: We can also use the Pythagorean Theorem to find x.

$(x + 2)^2 = 2^2 + 2^2 = 4 + 4 = 8$. So $x + 2 = \sqrt{8} = 2\sqrt{2}$ and so $x = 2\sqrt{2} - 2$, choice (C).

Also, if you are uncomfortable simplifying square roots, you can simply perform the computations in your calculator and compare with the numbers next to "approximately" in the answer choices.

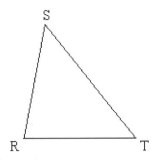

Note: Figure not drawn to scale.

148. In the triangle above, $RS = 7$ and $ST = 10$. Point U lies on RT between R and T so that $SU \perp RT$. Which of the following cannot be the length of SU?

(A) 3
(B) 4
(C) 5
(D) 6
(E) 8

*Let's draw SU.

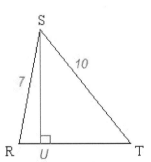

Note: Figure not drawn to scale.

Now just note that RS is the hypotenuse of triangle RSU. Thus SU must be less than 7. So SU cannot be 8, and the answer is choice (E).

For more information on this technique, see **Strategy 9** in **"The 32 Most Effective SAT Math Strategies."**

149. If the length of a rectangle is increased by 40%, and the width of the same rectangle is decreased by 40%, then the area of the rectangle is decreased by $x\%$. What is the value of x ?

* Let's start with a rectangle that has length and width both 10, so that the area of this rectangle is 100 (that is, we are starting with a 10 by 10 square). The length and width of the new rectangle are then 14 and 6, respectively. Therefore the new area is 14*6 = 84. This is a decrease of **16%**.

For more information on this technique, see **Strategy 4** in **"The 32 Most Effective SAT Math Strategies."**

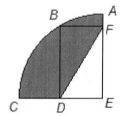

150. In the figure above, arc ABC is one quarter of a circle with center E, and radius 12. If the length plus the width of rectangle $BDEF$ is 16, then the perimeter of the shaded region is

   (A) $16 + 6\pi$
   (B) $20 + 6\pi$
   (C) $28 + 6\pi$
   (D) $2 + 12\pi$
   (E) $24 + 12\pi$

* It does not say "Figure not drawn to scale." So let's assume it is. Then CD = 6 because it looks like half the radius. Similarly DE = 6, and therefore EF = 16 − 6 = 10 (because the length plus the width of the rectangle is 16). Now EA is a radius, so FA = 12 − 10 = 2. EB (not drawn) is also a radius. So EB = 12. Since both diagonals of a rectangle are congruent, DF = 12. The circumference of a circle with radius is 12 is

$$C = 2\pi r = 2\pi(12) = 24\pi.$$

Arc AC is a quarter circle, and thus has length AC = 24π/4 = 6π.

Finally, we just add to get the perimeter.

CD + DF + FA + ABC = 6 + 12 + 2 + 6π = 20 + 6π, choice (B).

For more information on this technique, see **Strategy 6** in **"The 32 Most Effective SAT Math Strategies."**

Remark: Although the above method gives us the correct answer, the method of solution is actually **not** correct. Note that triangle DEF is a right triangle, and therefore should satisfy the Pythagorean Theorem. But $DE^2 + EF^2 = 6^2 + 10^2 = 136$. So DF should be approximately 11.66, and **not** 12. The error that we made was in assuming that CD = DE. Note that this error does not matter as far as getting the solution is concerned, but the more advanced student should try to solve this problem the correct way (not on the SAT, but at home for practice).

A correct solution for the advanced student: This is quite difficult, and is only included for completeness. Since the length plus the width of the rectangle is 16, if we let DE = x, then EF = 16 − x. Recall that DF is congruent to BE, and so DF = 12, the radius of the circle. By the Pythagorean Theorem, $x^2 + (16 - x)^2 = 12^2$. So $x^2 + 256 - 32x + x^2 = 144$. Simplifying this gives us $2x^2 - 32x + 112 = 0$. We divide through by 2 to get $x^2 - 16x + 56 = 0$. We can use the quadratic formula to solve for x.

$$x = (16 \pm \sqrt{(-16)^2 - 4(1)(56)})/2 = (16 \pm \sqrt{32})/2 = (16 \pm 4\sqrt{2})/2 = 8 \pm 2\sqrt{2}$$

We let DE = $x = 8 - 2\sqrt{2}$ so that EF = 16 − x = 16 − (8 − 2$\sqrt{2}$) = 8 + 2$\sqrt{2}$. So CD = 12 − (8 − 2$\sqrt{2}$) = 4 + 2$\sqrt{2}$ and FA = 12 − (8 + 2$\sqrt{2}$) = 4 − 2$\sqrt{2}$.

Finally we have CD + DF + FA + AC = (4 + 2$\sqrt{2}$) + 12 + (4 − 2$\sqrt{2}$) + 6π
= 20 + 6π, choice (B).

(See the original solution above to see where 6π comes from.)

Remark: We could have chosen x to be $8 + 2\sqrt{2}$. The solution would come out the same. The value of x that we chose matches the picture a little better.

151. In the xy – plane, line k has equation $y = \dfrac{2}{3}x + 7$, and line n has equation $y = \dfrac{1}{5}x + b$. If the lines intersect at the point with coordinates $(a, \dfrac{3}{2})$, what is the value of b ?

* We first find the value of a by substituting the given point into the first equation:

$$3/2 = 2/3 \,(a) + 7$$

Let's multiply each side of the equation by 6 to clear the denominators.

$$9 = 4a + 42$$

Subtracting 42 from each side of the equation yields

$$-33 = 4a$$

Thus,

$$a = -33/4.$$

So the point is (-33/4, 3/2).

We now plug this point into the second equation:

$$3/2 = 1/5 \,(-33/4) + b$$
$$3/2 = -33/20 + b$$

Let's multiply each side of the equation by 20 to clear the denominators.

$$30 = -33 + 20b.$$
$$63 = 20b$$

So b = 63/20 which is equal to **3.15**.

Remark: If you prefer, all of the algebra can be done in your calculator. This will allow you to avoid having to clear the denominators.

For example, for the equation

$$3/2 = 2/3 \ (a) + 7$$

you can simply type the following into your calculator to find the value of a:

$3 \div 2 - 7$ Enter $* \ 3 \div 2$ Enter

This will give a = -8.25.

You can find the value of b similarly.

152. In $\triangle ABC$, the length of side BC is 16 and the length of side AC is 27. What is the greatest possible integer length of side AB?

We use the **triangle rule** which says that the third side of a triangle is between the sum and difference of the other two sides. So we have that 27 - 16 < AB < 27 + 16. That is, 11 < AB < 43. Therefore the greatest possible integer length of side AB is **42**.

* A slightly quicker solution: For this particular question we actually only need that the third side of the triangle is less than the sum of the other two sides. So we have that AB < 27 + 16 = 43. Thus, AB = **42**.

For more information on this technique, see **Strategy 25** in **"The 32 Most Effective SAT Math Strategies.**

LEVEL 5: PROBABILITY AND STATISTICS

$$\frac{1}{x^3}, \frac{1}{x^2}, \frac{1}{x}, x, x^2, x^3$$

153. If $-1 < x < 0$, what is the median of the six numbers in the list above?

(A) $\dfrac{1}{x}$

(B) x^2

(C) $\dfrac{x^2(x+1)}{2}$

(D) $\dfrac{x(x^2+1)}{2}$

(E) $\dfrac{x^2+1}{2x}$

* Let's choose x = -0.5.

We use our calculator to compute the given expressions.

$1/x^3 = -8$ $1/x^2 = 4$ $1/x = -2$ $x = -0.5$ $x^2 = 0.25$ $x^3 = -0.125$

Now let's place them in increasing order.

-8, -2, -0.5, -0.125, 0.25, 4

The median is the average of -0.5 and -0.125, ie. it is **-0.3125**. Now let's substitute x = -0.5 into each answer choice.

(A) -2
(B) 0.25
(C) 0.0625
(D) -0.3125
(E) -1.25

142

Since (A), (B), (C) and (E) are incorrect we can eliminate them. Therefore the answer is choice (D).

Important note: (D) is **not** the correct answer simply because it is equal to -0.3125. It is correct because all four of the other choices are **not** -0.3125. **You absolutely must check all five choices!**

For more information on this technique, see **Strategy 4** in **"The 32 Most Effective SAT Math Strategies."**

154. The integers 1 through 5 are written on each of five cards. The cards are shuffled and one card is drawn at random. That card is then replaced, the cards are shuffled again and another card is drawn at random. This procedure is repeated one more time (for a total of three times). What is the probability that the sum of the numbers on the three cards drawn was 14 or 15?

   (A) $\dfrac{1}{125}$

   (B) $\dfrac{2}{125}$

   (C) $\dfrac{4}{125}$

   (D) $\dfrac{1}{25}$

   (E) $\dfrac{2}{25}$

* The total number of possibilities for the three cards is 5*5*5 = 125.

5 + 5 + 5 = 15
5 + 5 + 4 = 14
5 + 4 + 5 = 14
4 + 5 + 5 = 14

Thus there are 4 possibilities that give the desired sum. The probability is therefore 4/125, choice (C).

155. If $f = a + b + c + d + e$, what is the average (arithmetic mean) of a, b, c, d, e, and f in terms of f ?

(A) $\dfrac{f}{2}$

(B) $\dfrac{f}{3}$

(C) $\dfrac{f}{4}$

(D) $\dfrac{f}{5}$

(E) $\dfrac{f}{6}$

* The average of a, b, c, d, e, and f is

(a + b + c + d + e + f)/6 = (a + b + c + d + e + a + b + c + d + e)/6

= (2a + 2b + 2c + 2d + 2e)/6 = 2(a + b + c + d + e)/6 = 2f/6 = f/3.

This is choice (B).

Alternate solution by picking numbers: Let's let a = 1, b = 2, c = 3, d = 4, and e = 5. Then f = 15, and the average of a, b, c, d, e, and f is

(1+ 2 + 3 + 4 + 5 + 15)/6 = 30/6 = **5**. Put a nice big, dark circle around this number. Now plug in f = 15 to each answer choice.

(A) 7.5
(B) 5
(C) 3.75
(D) 3
(E) 2.5

Since (A), (C), (D) and (E) are incorrect we can eliminate them. Therefore the answer is choice (B).

Important note: (B) is **not** the correct answer simply because it is equal to 5. It is correct because all 4 of the other choices are **not** 5.

For more information on this technique, see **Strategy 4** in **"The 32 Most Effective SAT Math Strategies."**

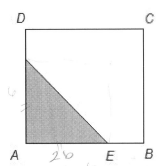

Note: Figure not drawn to scale.

156. In the figure above, $ABCD$ is a square, $AD = 6$, $EB = 6 - 2b$, and the triangle is isosceles. A point in square $ABCD$ is to be chosen at random. If the probability that the point will be in the shaded triangle is $\frac{1}{3}$, what is the value of b ?

    (A) $\sqrt{6}$
    (B) $\sqrt{10}$
    (C) $2\sqrt{6}$
    (D) $\sqrt{10}$
    (E) 6

* AE = 6 − (6 − 2b) = 6 − 6 + 2b = 2b. So the area of the triangle is

$$1/2 \ (2b)(2b) = 2b^2.$$

The area of the square is 6*6 = 36. Thus the probability of choosing a point in the triangle is $2b^2/36 = b^2/18$. We are given that this is equal to 1/3. We cross multiply and divide to get

$3b^2 = 18$. So $b^2 = 6$, and $b = \sqrt{6}$, choice (A).

157. A five digit number is to be formed using each of the digits 1, 2, 3, 4, and 5 exactly once. How many such numbers are there in which the digits 1 and 2 are not next to each other?

   (A) 36
   (B) 48
   (C) 60
   (D) 72
   (E) 120

Beginner Method: Let's start by thinking about where 1 can go. There are 2 cases:

1st Case: 1 is placed at an end. In this case, there are now 3 places where the 2 can go. After the 2 is placed, there are 3 places for the 3, then 2 places for the 4, and then 1 place for the 5. By the counting principle there are 2*3*3*2*1 = **36** ways to form the five digit number when the 1 is placed at either end (note that the first 2 comes from the fact that we have 2 choices for 1 – the far left or the far right).

2nd Case: 1 is not placed at an end. In this case, there are now 2 places where the 2 can go, and then the rest is the same as case 1. So again by the counting principle there are 3*2*3*2*1 = **36** ways to form the five digit number when the 1 is **not** placed at either end (note that the first 3 comes from the fact that we have 3 choices for 1 – each of the 3 middle positions).

So adding up the possibilities from cases 1 and 2, we get 36 + 36 = 72 possibilities all together, choice (D).

* Advanced Method: Let's first compute the number of ways to place the 1 and 2 with 1 to the left of 2. If the 1 is placed in the leftmost position, then there are 3 places to put the 2 to the right of the 1. If the 1 is placed in the next position to the right, then there are 2 places to put the 2 to the right of the 1. If the 1 is placed in the middle position, then there is 1 place to put the 2 to the right of the 1. Therefore there are 3 + 2 + 1 = 6 places to put the 1 and 2 with 1 < 2. By symmetry, there are 6 places to put the 1 and the 2 with 2 < 1. So all together there are 12 places to put the 1 and 2. Once the 1 and 2 are placed, there are 3 places to put the 3, then 2 places to put the 4, and 1 place to put the 5. By the counting principle the answer is 12*3*2*1 = **72**.

158. Let a, b and c be numbers with $a < b < c$ such that the average of a and b is 2, the average of b and c is 4, and the average of a and c is 3. What is the average of a, b and c?

* We change the averages to sums using the following simple formula.

Sum = Average * Number

So a + b = 4
b + c = 8
a + c = 6

Adding these 3 equations gives us 2a + 2b + 2c = 18, so that a + b + c = 9. Finally, we divide by 3 to get that the average of a, b and c is 9/3 = **3**.

159. A group of students take a test and the average score is 65. One more student takes the test and receives a score of 92 increasing the average score of the group to 68. How many students were in the initial group?

* Let n be the number of students in the initial group. We change the average to a sum using the following simple formula.

Sum = Average * Number

So the initial Sum is 65n.

When we take into account the new student, we can find the new sum in two different ways.

(1) We can add the new score to the old sum to get 65n + 92.

(2) We can compute the new sum directly using the simple formula above to get 68(n + 1) = 68n + 68.

We now set these equal to each other and solve for n:

$$65n + 92 = 68n + 68$$
$$24 = 3n$$
$$n = \textbf{8}.$$

For more information on this technique, see **Strategy 20** in **"The 32 Most Effective SAT Math Strategies."**

160. How many integers between 3000 and 4000 have digits that are all different and that increase from left to right?

* Let's form a list:

3456	3567
7	8
8	9
9	78
67	9
8	89
9	678
78	9
9	89
89	789

There are **20** integers in this list.

Remarks:

(1) Notice that we only wrote down the necessary information when forming our list. For example, the second entry was just written "7" instead of "3457." This will save a substantial amount of time.

(2) A clear and definite pattern was used in forming this list. In this case the list was written in increasing order. This will minimize the risk of duplicating or leaving out entries.

For more information on this technique, see **Strategy 21** in **"The 32 Most Effective SAT Math Strategies."**

SUPPLEMENTAL PROBLEMS
QUESTIONS

Full solutions to these problems are available for free download here:

www.thesatmathprep.com/320SATprmT1.html

LEVEL 1: NUMBER THEORY

1. Which of the following numbers is greater than 0.216?

    (A) 0.2106
    (B) 0.215
    (C) 0.2156
    (D) 0.2159
    (E) 0.2161

2. What is the greatest positive integer that is a divisor of 14, 49, and 63?

    (A) 14
    (B) 7
    (C) 3
    (D) 2
    (E) 1

3. A positive integer is called a palindrome if it reads the same forward as it does backward. For example, 2442 is a palindrome. What is the smallest palindrome greater than 2513?

    (A) 2112
    (B) 2514
    (C) 2525
    (D) 2552
    (E) 2553

4. Which of the following numbers is between $\frac{1}{8}$ and $\frac{1}{7}$?

    (A) 0.13
    (B) 0.15
    (C) 0.17
    (D) 0.19
    (E) 0.21

5. Which of the following numbers disproves the statement "A number that is divisible by 6 and 12 is also divisible by 18"?

    (A) 18
    (B) 36
    (C) 48
    (D) 72
    (E) 108

6. $(4+5)^2 =$

7. If 4.56 is rounded to the nearest tenth and the result is doubled, what is the final result?

8. Three consecutive integers are listed in increasing order. If their sum is 603, what is the third integer in the list?

LEVEL 1: ALGEBRA AND FUNCTIONS

9. If $1+x+2+x+3=x+1+x+2+x$, what is the value of x?

    (A) 1
    (B) 2
    (C) 3
    (D) 4
    (E) 5

10. If $a + b = 12$ and $a = 5$, then $4b =$

    (A) 12
    (B) 21
    (C) 24
    (D) 28
    (E) 35

11. If Robert drove a miles in b hours, which of the following represents his average speed, in miles per hour?

    (A) $\dfrac{a}{b}$

    (B) $\dfrac{b}{a}$

    (C) $\dfrac{1}{ab}$

    (D) ab
    (E) $a^2 b$

12. If $3y - 18 = 15$, then $y - 6 =$

    (A) 30
    (B) 20
    (C) 15
    (D) 10
    (E) 5

13. If $4^2 = 2^z$, then $z =$

    (A) 4
    (B) 3
    (C) 2
    (D) 1
    (E) 0

14. If $a = \dfrac{7}{b}$ and $c = 8a$, what is the value of c when $b = 42$?

15. If $(c+2)(15-6) = 21$, then $5c =$

16. If $7(x-5) = 6(x-4)$, what is the value of x ?

Level 1: Geometry

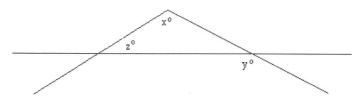

Note: Figure not drawn to scale.

17. In the figure above, if $y = 130$ and $z = 55$, what is the value of x ?

    (A) 15
    (B) 30
    (C) 50
    (D) 75
    (E) 130

18. If the degree measures of the three angles of a triangle are $60°$, $z°$ and $z°$, what is the value of z ?

    (A) 60
    (B) 65
    (C) 70
    (D) 75
    (E) 80

19. The volume of a rectangular box is 6 cubic inches. If the width of the box is 14 inches and the height is $\frac{1}{7}$ inch, what is the length?

    (A) $\frac{1}{14}$ inch

    (B) $\frac{1}{7}$ inch

    (C) 1 inch

    (D) 3 inches

    (E) 4 inches

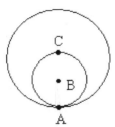

20. In the figure above, A, B, and C lie on the same line. B Is the center of the smaller circle, and C is the center of the larger circle. If the radius of the smaller circle is 7, what is the diameter of the larger circle?

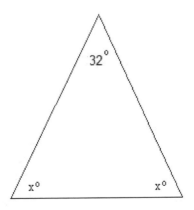

21. In the triangle above, what is the value of x ?

153

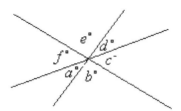

Note: Figure not drawn to scale.

22. In the figure above, three lines intersect at a point. If $a = 27$ and $c = 61$, what is the value of e ?

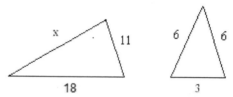

Note: Figure not drawn to scale.

23. If the perimeter of the triangle on the left is three times the perimeter of the triangle on the right, what is the value of x ?

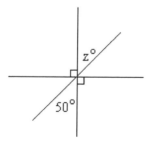

24. In the figure above, what is the value of z ?

LEVEL 1: PROBABILITY AND STATISTICS

25. The average (arithmetic mean) of four numbers is 100. If three of the numbers are 60, 70 and 140, what is the fourth number?

   (A) 90
   (B) 100
   (C) 110
   (D) 120
   (E) 130

26. A menu lists 8 meals and 3 drinks. How many different meal-drink combinations are possible from this menu?

   (A) 24
   (B) 12
   (C) 11
   (D) 8
   (E) 3

$$3, 4, 5, 6, 7, 8, 9, 10, 11$$

27. If a number is selected at random from the list above, what is the probability that it will be less than 7?

   (A) $\dfrac{2}{9}$
   (B) $\dfrac{1}{3}$
   (C) $\dfrac{4}{9}$
   (D) $\dfrac{2}{3}$
   (E) 1

28. There are exactly 17 coins in a bag. There are 6 pennies, 4 nickels, 5 dimes, and the rest are quarters. If one coin is selected at random from the bag, what is the probability that the coin is a quarter?

29. Fred's math class has a homework list of 7 algebra problems and 4 geometry problems. Fred will select one algebra problem and one geometry problem from the list to complete the homework assignment. How many different choices of an algebra problem and a geometry problem are possible?

30. The average (arithmetic mean) of eight numbers is 250. If the sum of seven of the numbers is 1463, what is the eighth number?

31. In a jar there are exactly 56 marbles, each of which is yellow, purple, or blue. The probability of randomly selecting a yellow marble from the jar is $\frac{2}{7}$, and the probability of randomly selecting a purple marble from the jar is $\frac{3}{7}$. How many marbles in the jar are blue?

32. Joe, Mike, Phil, John and Fred own a total of 138 CDs. If John owns 38 of them, what is the average (arithmetic mean) number of CDs owned by Joe, Mike, Phil and Fred?

LEVEL 2: NUMBER THEORY

33. Starting with a blue tile, colored tiles are placed in a row according to the pattern blue, green, yellow, orange, red, purple. If this pattern is repeated, what is the color of the 73rd tile?

   (A) Blue
   (B) Green
   (C) Yellow
   (D) Orange
   (E) Red

34. If k is an even integer, what is the smallest even integer greater than k ?

   (A) $k+3$
   (B) $k+2$
   (C) $k+1$
   (D) $2(k+1)$
   (E) $2(k+1)+3$

35. A room has 2000 square feet of surface that needs to be painted. If 3 gallons of paint will cover 520 square feet, what is the least whole number of gallons that must be purchased in order to have enough paint to cover the entire surface?

   (A) 8
   (B) 9
   (C) 10
   (D) 11
   (E) 12

36. A piece of cable x feet in length is cut into exactly 6 pieces, each 2 feet 3 inches in length. What is the value of x ?

   (A) $12\frac{2}{3}$
   (B) 13
   (C) $13\frac{1}{2}$
   (D) $13\frac{2}{3}$
   (E) 14

157

37. In September, Maria was able to type 30 words per minute. In October she was able to type 42 words per minute. By what percent did Jennifer's speed increase from September to October?

    (A) 12%
    (B) 18%
    (C) 30%
    (D) 40%
    (E) 42%

20, 59, 30, 89, 45, ...

38. In the sequence above, 20 is the first term and each term thereafter is obtained by using the following rules.

-   If the previous term is even, multiply it by 3 and then subtract 1.
-   If the previous term is odd, add 1 to it and then divide by 2.

What is the eighth term of the sequence?

39. A copy machine makes 2000 copies per hour. At this rate, in how many <u>minutes</u> can the copy machine produce 800 copies?

40. The ratio of 17 to 3 is equal to the ratio of 102 to what number?

LEVEL 2: ALGEBRA AND FUNCTIONS

41. If $3x + 7 = 24$, then $3x - 7 =$

    (A) 8
    (B) 9
    (C) 10
    (D) 11
    (E) 12

158

42. The number a is 5 less than 7 times the number b. The sum of a and b is 14. Which of the following pairs of equations could be used to find the values of a and b?

    (A) $a = 7(b-5)$
         $a+b = 14$

    (B) $a = 5(7-b)$
         $a = 14-b$

    (C) $a = 7(b-5)$
         $a = 14-b$

    (D) $a = 7b-5$
         $a+b = 14$

    (E) $a = 5-7b$
         $a+b = 14$

43. Which of the following is an expression for 25 less than the product of y and 7?

    (A) $7y-25$
    (B) $25-7y$
    (C) $(y+7)-25$
    (D) $7(y-25)$
    (E) y^7-25

44. If $\dfrac{y}{z} = -3$, then $y+3z =$

    (A) -1
    (B) 0
    (C) 1
    (D) y
    (E) z

45. If $7x + y = 6$ and $5x + y = 2$, what is the value of $6x + y$?

    (A) -8
    (B) 4
    (C) 6
    (D) 12
    (E) 18

46. If 3 less than x is 1 more than 6, what is the value of x?

47. If $6^{x+1} = 7776$, what is the value of x?

48. If $6x - 2y = 11$, what is the value of $4(6x - 2y)$?

LEVEL 2: GEOMETRY

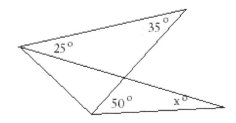

49. In the figure above, what is the value of x?

    (A) 10
    (B) 15
    (C) 20
    (D) 25
    (E) 30

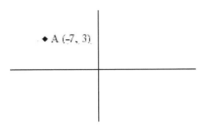

50. In the figure above, a line is to be drawn through point A so that it never crosses the y-axis. Through which of the following points must the line pass?

    (A) $(7, 3)$
    (B) $(7, -3)$
    (C) $(-7, -3)$
    (D) $(3, 7)$
    (E) $(-3, -7)$

51. C is the midpoint of line segment AB, and D and E are the midpoints of AC and CB, respectively. If the length of DE is 7, what is the length of AB ?

    (A) 3.5
    (B) 7
    (C) 10.5
    (D) 14
    (E) 17.5

52. In an xy coordinate system, which point lies in the interior of a circle with center (0, 0) and radius 4?

    (A) (1, -4)
    (B) (-2, -3)
    (C) (-4, 1)
    (D) (0, 4)
    (E) (4, 4)

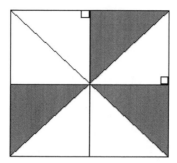

53. What percent of the square above is shaded?

    (A) 25%

    (B) $33\dfrac{1}{3}$%

    (C) $37\dfrac{1}{2}$%

    (D) 50%

    (E) $62\dfrac{2}{3}$%

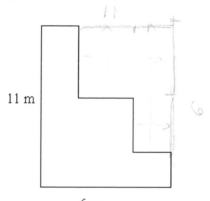

11 m

6 m

Note: Figure not drawn to scale.

54. What is the perimeter, in meters, of the figure above?

55. If the sum of the areas of two congruent squares is 72, what is the length of a side of each square?

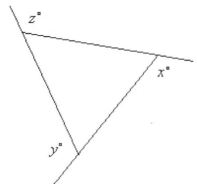

Note: Figure not drawn to scale.

56. In the figure above, what is the value of $x + y + z$?

LEVEL 2: PROBABILITY AND STATISTICS

57. The average (arithmetic mean) of three numbers is 72. If one of the numbers is 21, what is the sum of the other two?

 (A) 71
 (B) 92
 (C) 177
 (D) 183
 (E) 195

58. What is the average (arithmetic mean) of $11 - k$, 11, and $11 + k$?

 (A) 3
 (B) 11
 (C) 15
 (D) $3 + \dfrac{k}{3}$
 (E) $11 + \dfrac{k}{3}$

163

59. The average (arithmetic mean) of 9, 15, 18, and y is 20. What is the value of y ?

    (A) 25
    (B) 36
    (C) 38
    (D) 39
    (E) 67

$$16, 21, 13, 12, 3, 19, 2, 5, 22, 36, b$$

60. If b is the median of the 11 numbers listed above, which of the following could be the value of b ?

    (A) 4
    (B) 8
    (C) 14
    (D) 17
    (E) 18

61. The average (arithmetic mean) of ten numbers is 77. If an eleventh number, 22, is added to the group, what is the average of the eleven numbers?

62. A is a set of numbers whose average (arithmetic mean) is 11. B is a set that is generated by doubling each number in A. What is the average of the numbers in set B ?

63. The average (arithmetic mean) of 7, 11, 15, and z is z . What is the value of z ?

64. Of the marbles in a jar, 14 are green. Joseph randomly takes one marble out of the jar. If the probability is $\dfrac{7}{8}$ that the marble he chooses is green, how many marbles are in the jar?

LEVEL 3: NUMBER THEORY

65. If an integer n is divisible by 5, 7, 25, and 35, what is the next larger integer divisible by these numbers?

   (A) $n+50$
   (B) $n+75$
   (C) $n+125$
   (D) $n+150$
   (E) $n+175$

66. If x and y are negative odd integers, which of the following must be a negative odd integer?

   (A) $x+y$
   (B) $x-y$
   (C) $2x+y$
   (D) $2x-y$
   (E) $\dfrac{x+y}{2}$

67. How many <u>seconds</u> are required for a bicycle to go 3 miles at a constant speed of 6 miles per hour?

   (A) 3600
   (B) 3000
   (C) 2400
   (D) 1800
   (E) 1200

68. The cost of 7 hats is d dollars. At this rate, what is the cost, in dollars of 63 hats?

   (A) $\dfrac{9d}{7}$

   (B) $\dfrac{d}{63}$

   (C) $\dfrac{63}{d}$

   (D) $9d$

   (E) $63d$

69. When 407 is divided by 9, the remainder is r, and when 234 is divided by 7, the remainder is s. What is the value of rs?

70. What is the smallest positive integer divisible by 3, 5, 7, and 35?

71. What percent of 70 is 14? (Disregard the percent symbol when gridding in your answer.)

72. The quantity (3×4^{11}) is how many times the quantity (3×4^{6})?

LEVEL 3: ALGEBRA AND FUNCTIONS

73. In the exact middle of a certain book, when the page numbers on the facing pages, x and $x+1$, are multiplied together, the product is 272. If all the pages are numbered in order, how many numbered pages are in the book?

   (A) 30
   (B) 32
   (C) 34
   (D) 36
   (E) 38

74. If x is $\dfrac{3}{5}$ of y and y is $\dfrac{5}{7}$ of z, what is the value of $\dfrac{z}{x}$?

   (A) $\dfrac{1}{4}$

   (B) $\dfrac{3}{7}$

   (C) $\dfrac{5}{4}$

   (D) $\dfrac{10}{7}$

   (E) $\dfrac{7}{3}$

75. If $\dfrac{9}{x} + \dfrac{7}{8} = \dfrac{85}{56}$, what is the value of x?

   (A) -14
   (B) -7
   (C) 2
   (D) 7
   (E) 14

76. If $20x + 36y = 56$, what is the value of $5x + 9y$?

   (A) 7
   (B) 8
   (C) 14
   (D) 15
   (E) 30

167

77. The function k is defined by $k(x) = 3x^2 + bx - 2$, where b is a constant. In the xy-plane, the graph of $y = k(x)$ crosses the x-axis where $x = 2$. What is the value of b?

    (A) 5
    (B) 2.5
    (C) 0
    (D) -2.5
    (E) -5

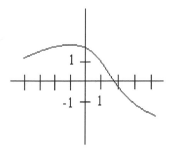

78. The figure above shows the graph of the function f. Which of the following is less than $f(2)$?

    (A) $f(-4)$
    (B) $f(-3)$
    (C) $f(-1)$
    (D) $f(1)$
    (E) $f(3)$

79. If $7^x = 5$, then $7^{4x} =$

80. Let g be a function such that $g(x) = |3x| - k$ where k is a constant. If $g(4) = -2$, what is the value of $g(-5)$?

168

Level 3: Geometry

81. The volume of a right circular cylinder is 216π cubic centimeters. If the height and base radius of the cylinder are equal, what is the base diameter of the cylinder?

    (A) 4 centimeters
    (B) 6 centimeters
    (C) 10 centimeters
    (D) 12 centimeters
    (E) 36 centimeters

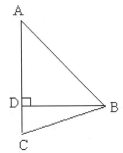

Note: Figure not drawn to scale.

82. Triangle ABC has the same area as a rectangle with sides of lengths 3 and 11. If the length of BD is 6, what is the length of AC?

    (A) 8
    (B) 9
    (C) 10
    (D) 11
    (E) 12

83. In the xy-coordinate plane, line n passes through the points (0,3) and (-1,0). If line m is perpendicular to line n, what is the slope of line m?

   (A) - 3
   (B) $-\dfrac{1}{3}$
   (C) 1
   (D) $\dfrac{1}{3}$
   (E) 3

84. Point O lies in plane P. How many circles are there in plane P that have center O and an area of 25π centimeters?

   (A) None
   (B) One
   (C) Two
   (D) Three
   (E) More than three

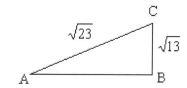

Note: Figure not drawn to scale.

85. In right triangle ABC above, what is the length of side AB to the nearest tenth?

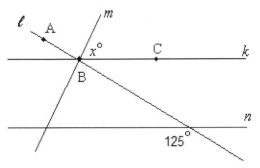

Note: Figure not drawn to scale.

86. In the figure above, line k is parallel to line n. If line m bisects angle ABC, what is the value of x?

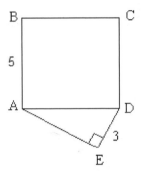

87. In the figure above, $ABCD$ is a square. What is the area of triangle AED?

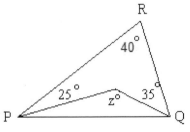

Note: Figure not drawn to scale.

88. In triangle PQR above, what is the value of z?

171

LEVEL 3: PROBABILITY AND STATISTICS

89. A chemist is testing 6 different liquids. For each test, the chemist chooses 3 of the liquids and mixes them together. What is the least number of tests that must be done so that every possible combination of liquids is tested?

(A) 5
(B) 10
(C) 15
(D) 20
(E) 25

90. There are y bricks in a row. If one brick is to be selected at random, the probability that it will <u>not</u> be cracked is $\frac{6}{7}$. In terms of y, how many of the bricks are cracked?

(A) $\dfrac{y}{7}$

(B) $\dfrac{5y}{7}$

(C) $\dfrac{7y}{5}$

(D) $\dfrac{12y}{7}$

(E) $7y$

TEST GRADES OF STUDENTS IN MATH CLASS

Test Grade	65	81	84	92	100
Number of students with that grade	1	8	6	2	4

91. The test grades of the 21 students in a math class are shown in the chart above. What is the median test grade for the class?

    (A) 65
    (B) 81
    (C) 82.5
    (D) 84
    (E) 92

92. A group of dogs are fed Brand A and Brand B dog food only. Of these dogs, 4 dogs eat Brand A and 9 dogs eat Brand B. If 2 of the dogs that eat Brand B also eat Brand A, how many dogs are in the group?

93. The average (arithmetic mean) of eleven numbers is 15. When a twelfth number is added, the average of the twelve numbers is 14. What is the twelfth number?

94. Set A contains only the integers 0 through 157 inclusive. If a number is selected at random from A, what is the probability that the number selected will be less than 79?

95. Seven different books are to be stacked in a pile. One book is chosen for the bottom of the pile. In how many different orders can the remaining books be placed on the stack?

96. The average of x, y, z, and w is 8 and the average of z and w is 5. What is the average of x and y?

LEVEL 4: NUMBER THEORY

97. If the ratio of two positive integers is 5 to 4, which of the following statements about these integers CANNOT be true?

   (A) Their sum is an odd integer.
   (B) Their sum is an even integer.
   (C) Their product is divisible by 7.
   (D) Their product is an even integer.
   (E) Their product is an odd integer.

98. A positive integer is called a palindrome if it reads the same forward as it does backward. For example, 2442 is a palindrome. How many four-digit palindromes are there?

   (A) 19
   (B) 20
   (C) 90
   (D) 100
   (E) 810

99. The sum of 8 positive even integers is 158. If each of these integers is distinct, what is the greatest possible value of one of these integers?

   (A) 106
   (B) 104
   (C) 102
   (D) 100
   (E) 98

100. A person cuts a cake into n equal pieces and eats five pieces. In terms of n, what percent of the cake has been eaten?

    (A) 500%

    (B) $\dfrac{500}{n}\%$

    (C) $\dfrac{100n}{5}\%$

    (D) $\dfrac{n-5}{100}\%$

    (E) $\dfrac{100(n-5)}{n}\%$

101. If m, and n are distinct positive integers such that n is divisible by m, and m is divisible by 3, which of the following statements must be true?

       I. n is divisible by 3.
      II. $n = 3m$.
     III. n has more than 3 positive factors.

    (A) I only
    (B) III only
    (C) I and II only
    (D) I and III only
    (E) I, II, and III

102. Set A consists of k integers, and the difference between the greatest integer in A and the least integer in A is 500. A new set of k integers, set B, is formed by multiplying each integer in A by 6 and then subtracting 10 from the product. What is the difference between the greatest integer in B and the least integer in B?

    (A) 500
    (B) 2490
    (C) 2500
    (D) 2990
    (E) 3000

103. If k is divided by 8, the remainder is 3. What is the remainder if $3k$ is divided by 8?

104. A mixture is made by combining a red liquid and a blue liquid so that the ratio of the red liquid to the blue liquid is 19 to 4 by weight. How many liters of the blue liquid are needed to make a 552 liter mixture?

LEVEL 4: ALGEBRA AND FUNCTIONS

105. If $x^2 = 4$ and $y^2 = 7$, then $(2x+y)^2$ could equal which of the following?

   (A) 23
   (B) 65
   (C) 121
   (D) $23 - 8\sqrt{7}$
   (E) $65 + 8\sqrt{7}$

106. If $y = 3^x$, which of the following expressions is equivalent to $9^x - 3^{x+2}$ for all positive integer values of x?

   (A) $3y - 3$
   (B) y^2
   (C) $y^2 - y$
   (D) $y^2 - 3y$
   (E) $y^2 - 9y$

107. Positive integers a, b, and c satisfy the equations $a^{-b} = \dfrac{1}{64}$ and $b^c = 216$. If $a < b$, what is the value of $2a + b - c$?

    (A) 6
    (B) 7
    (C) 8
    (D) 9
    (E) 10

108. A small hotel has 15 rooms which are all occupied. If each room is occupied by either one or two guests and there are 27 guests in total, how many rooms are occupied by two guests?

109. Let $\bullet$ be defined by $x \bullet y = y^x$. If $a = x \bullet 2$, $b = y \bullet 2$, and $x + y = 3$, what is the value of ab?

110. Let the function f be defined for all values of x by $f(x) = x(x+1)$. If k is a positive number and $f(k+5) = 72$, what is the value of k?

111. For any real numbers r and s such that $r \neq s$, let $r \propto s$ be defined by $r \propto s = \dfrac{r+s}{r-s}$. If $r + s = 49$ and $r \propto s = 7$, what is the value of s?

112. For all numbers a and b, let $a \lozenge b = a^2 - 2ab^3$. What is the value of $\left| (4 \lozenge 1) \lozenge 2 \right|$?

177

LEVEL 4: GEOMETRY

113. Point A is a vertex of a 7-sided polygon. The polygon has 7 sides of equal length and 7 angles of equal measure. When all possible diagonals are drawn from point A in the polygon, how many triangles are formed?

    (A) One
    (B) Two
    (C) Three
    (D) Four
    (E) Five

114. If $a > 1$, what is the slope of the line in the xy-plane that passes through the points (a, a^3) and (a^2, a^5)?

    (A) $-a^3 + 6a^2$
    (B) $-a^3 + a^2$
    (C) $-a^3 - a^2$
    (D) $a^3 - a^2$
    (E) $a^3 + a^2$

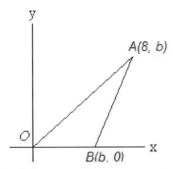

Note: Figure not drawn to scale.

115. In the xy-plane above, the area of triangle OAB is 32. What is the value of b ?

    (A) 8
    (B) 12
    (C) 16
    (D) 32
    (E) 64

116. A container in the shape of a right circular cylinder has an inside base diameter of 12 centimeters and an inside height of 10 centimeters. This cylinder is completely filled with fluid. All of the fluid is then poured into a second right circular cylinder with a smaller inside base diameter of 8 centimeters. What must be the minimum inside height, in centimeters, of the second container?

117. Points P and Q are on the surface of a sphere that has a volume of 972π cubic meters. What is the greatest possible length, in meters, of line segment PQ? (The volume of a sphere with radius r is $V = \dfrac{4}{3}\pi r^3$.)

179

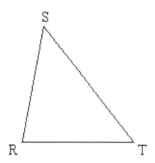

Note: Figure not drawn to scale.

118. In the triangle above, $RS = RT = 15$ and $ST = 8$. What is the area of the triangle to the nearest tenth?

119. In the xy-plane, line ℓ is the graph of $5x + ky = 9$, where k is a constant. The graph of $20x + 16y = 11$ is parallel to line ℓ. What is the value of k?

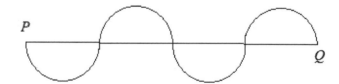

120. In the figure above, the diameters of the four semicircles are equal and lie on line segment PQ. If the length of line segment PQ is $\dfrac{64}{\pi}$, what is the length of the curve from P to Q?

LEVEL 4: PROBABILITY AND STATISTICS

121. If the average (arithmetic mean) of a, b, and 26 is 16, what is the average of a and b?

   (A) $5\frac{1}{2}$

   (B) 8
   (C) 11
   (D) 22
   (E) It cannot be determined from the information given.

122. Twenty one people were playing a game. 6 people scored 10 points, 5 people scored 30 points, 4 people scored 50 points, 3 people scored 70 points, 2 people scored 90 points, and 1 person scored 100 points. Which of the following correctly shows the order of the median, mode and average (arithmetic mean) of the 21 scores?

   (A) average < median< mode
   (B) average < mode < median
   (C) median < mode < average
   (D) median < average < mode
   (E) mode < median < average

123. The average (arithmetic mean) of 5 numbers is x. If one of the numbers is y, what is the average of the remaining 4 numbers in terms of x and y?

   (A) $\dfrac{x}{5}$

   (B) $5x - y$

   (C) $\dfrac{4x - y}{5}$

   (D) $\dfrac{5x - y}{4}$

   (E) $\dfrac{5y - x}{4}$

124. An urn contains a number of marbles of which 63 are green, 15 are purple, and the remainder are orange. If the probability of picking an orange marble from this urn at random is $\frac{1}{3}$, how many orange marbles are in the urn?

    (A) 13
    (B) 26
    (C) 39
    (D) 78
    (E) 244

125. Exactly 5 actors try out for the 5 parts in a movie. If each actor can perform any one part and no one will perform more than one part, how many different assignments of actors are possible?

126. A wall is to be painted one color with a stripe of a different color running through the middle. If 8 different colors are available, how many color combinations are possible?

127. A pet store has a white dog, a black dog, and a grey dog. The store also has three cats – one white, one black, and one grey – and three birds – one white, one black, and one grey. Jonathon wants to buy one dog, one cat, and one bird. How many different possibilities does he have?

128. Any 2 points determine a line. If there are 10 points in a plane, no 3 of which lie on the same line, how many lines are determined by pairs of these 10 points?

LEVEL 5: NUMBER THEORY

129. In an empty square field, k rows of k trees are planted so that the whole field is filled with trees. If n of these trees lie along the boundary of the field, which of the following is equal to n?

   (A) $k^2 - (k-3)^2$
   (B) $k^2 - (k-2)^2$
   (C) $k^2 - (k-1)^2$
   (D) $4k - 3$
   (E) $4k - 2$

130. If x and y are integers and $x^2 y + xy^2$ is even, which of the following statements must be true?

   I. x is even
   II. xy is even
   III. $x + y$ is even

   (A) None
   (B) I only
   (C) III only
   (D) I and III only
   (E) I, II, and III

131. If $a^{14}b^{15}c^{16}d^{17} > 0$, which of the following products must be positive?

   (A) ab
   (B) ac
   (C) bc
   (D) ad
   (E) bd

183

132. If $a_k = 5 + 5^2 + 5^3 + 5^4 + \cdots + 5^k$, for which of the following values of k will a_k be divisible by 10?

    (A) 37
    (B) 51
    (C) 75
    (D) 88
    (E) 91

133. If n is a positive integer and $k = (n^3 - n)^2$, which of the following statements about k must be true for all values of n?

    I. k is a multiple of 3
    II. k is a multiple of 4
    III. k is a multiple of 36

    (A) I only
    (B) II only
    (C) III only
    (D) I and III only
    (E) I, II, and III

134. How many positive integers less than 3,000 are multiples of 13 and are equal to 3 times an even integer?

135. In how many of the integers from 1 to 150 does the digit 4 appear at least once?

136. In Steve's math class, 12 students play the piano and 17 students play the guitar. If a total of 19 students play only one of these two instruments, how many students play both instruments?

LEVEL 5: ALGEBRA AND FUNCTIONS

137. For how many integers n is $(7n-26)(5n+11)$ a negative number?

    (A) None
    (B) Two
    (C) Four
    (D) Six
    (E) Eight

$$x = 25z$$
$$y = 25z^2 + 3$$

138. If $z > 0$ in the equations above, what is y in terms of x?

    (A) $\dfrac{1}{25}x^2 + 1$

    (B) $\dfrac{1}{25}x^2 + 2$

    (C) $\dfrac{1}{25}x^2 + 3$

    (D) $\dfrac{1}{5}x^2 + 2$

    (E) $x^2 + 3$

139. If a and b are positive integers, which of the following is equivalent to $(5a)^{3b} - (5a)^{2b}$?

    (A) $(5a)^b$
    (B) $5^b(a^3 - a^2)$
    (C) $(5a)^{2b}[(5a)^{3b} - 1]$
    (D) $(5a)^{2b}(25a - 1)$
    (E) $(5a)^{2b}[(5a)^b - 1]$

$$k = a - b + 16$$
$$k = b - c - 7$$
$$k = c - d - 9$$
$$k = d - e + 12$$
$$k = e - a - 2$$

140. In the system of equations above, what is the value of k ?

    (A) 1
    (B) 2
    (C) 3
    (D) 4
    (E) 5

141. If $x^2 - y^2 = 10 - k - 3k^2$, and $x - y = 5 - 3k$, what is $x + y$ in terms of k ?

    (A) $k - 2$
    (B) $(k - 2)^2$
    (C) $k + 2$
    (D) $(k + 2)^2$
    (E) $k^2 - 4$

x	5	10	15
$g(x)$	4	a	10

x	7	14	28
$h(x)$	2	b	14

142. The tables above show some values for the functions g and h. If g and h are linear functions, what is the value of $5a - 2b$?

143. Let g be a function such that $g(x) = k(x-7)(x+7)$ where k is a nonzero constant. If $g(b-5.3) = 0$ and $b > 0$, what is the value of b?

$$(x-6)(x-2n) = x^2 - 8nx + k$$

144. In the equation above, n and k are constants. If the equation is true for all values of x, what is the value of k?

LEVEL 5: GEOMETRY

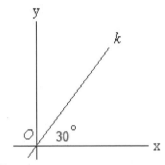

Note: Figure not drawn to scale.

145. In the figure above, what is the equation of line k?

(A) $y = \dfrac{x}{2}$

(B) $y = \dfrac{x}{\sqrt{2}}$

(C) $y = \dfrac{x}{\sqrt{3}}$

(D) $y = \sqrt{2}x$

(E) $y = \sqrt{3}x$

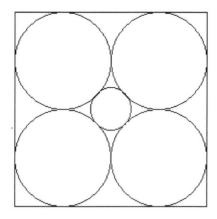

146. In the figure above, each of the four large circles is tangent to two of the other large circles, the small circle, and two sides of the square. If the diameter of each of the large circles is 10, what is the <u>radius</u> of the small circle?

    (A) $5\sqrt{2}$

    (B) 5

    (C) $5\sqrt{2}-5$

    (D) $\dfrac{5}{2}$

    (E) $5\sqrt{2}-1$

147. The lengths of the sides of an isosceles triangle are 22, n, and n. If n is an integer, what is the smallest possible perimeter of the triangle?

    (A) 30

    (B) 31

    (C) 32

    (D) 34

    (E) 46

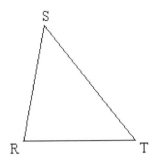

Note: Figure not drawn to scale.

148. In the triangle above, $RS = 4$ and $ST = 6$. Point U lies on RT between R and T so that $SU \perp RT$. Which of the following can be the length of SU?

    (A) 3
    (B) 4
    (C) 5
    (D) 6
    (E) 8

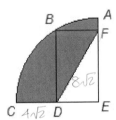

Note: Figure not drawn to scale.

149. In the figure above, arc ABC is one quarter of a circle with center E and radius $8\sqrt{2}$. If the length plus the width of rectangle $BDEF$ is 16, then the area of the shaded region is

    (A) $32\pi - 32$
    (B) $32\pi - 16$
    (C) $32\pi - 8$
    (D) $32\pi + 16$
    (E) $32\pi + 32$

150. If the length of a rectangle is increased by 60%, and the width of the same rectangle is decreased by 50%, then the area of the rectangle is decreased by $x\%$. What is the value of x?

151. In the xy-plane, line k has equation $y = \dfrac{12}{7}x + b$, and line n has equation $y = \dfrac{3}{2}x + 4$. If the lines intersect at the point with coordinates $(a, \dfrac{9}{4})$, what is the value of b?

152. The lengths of the sides of a triangle are x, 12, and 23, where x is the shortest side. If the triangle is not isosceles, what is a possible value of x?

LEVEL 5: PROBABILITY AND STATISTICS

$$\frac{1}{x^3}, \frac{1}{x^2}, \frac{1}{x}, x^2, x^3$$

153. If $-1 < x < 0$, what is the median of the five numbers in the list above?

(A) $\dfrac{1}{x^3}$

(B) $\dfrac{1}{x^2}$

(C) $\dfrac{1}{x}$

(D) x^2

(E) x^3

154. The integers 1 through 7 are written on each of seven cards. The cards are shuffled and one card is drawn at random. That card is then replaced, the cards are shuffled again and another card is drawn at random. This procedure is repeated one more time (for a total of three times). What is the probability that the sum of the numbers on the three cards drawn was 20 or 21?

(A) $\dfrac{1}{343}$

(B) $\dfrac{2}{343}$

(C) $\dfrac{4}{343}$

(D) $\dfrac{1}{49}$

(E) $\dfrac{2}{49}$

155. If $g = a+b+c+d+e+f$, what is the average (arithmetic mean) of a, b, c, d, e, f and g in terms of g?

(A) $\dfrac{3g}{7}$

(B) $\dfrac{2g}{5}$

(C) $\dfrac{g}{3}$

(D) $\dfrac{2g}{7}$

(E) $\dfrac{g}{4}$

191

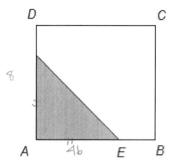

Note: Figure not drawn to scale.

156. In the figure above, $ABCD$ is a square, $AD = 8$, $EB = 8 - 4b$, and the triangle is isosceles. A point in square $ABCD$ is to be chosen at random. If the probability that the point will be in the shaded triangle is $\frac{1}{4}$, what is the value of b ?

    (A) $\sqrt{2}$
    (B) $\sqrt{3}$
    (C) $2\sqrt{2}$
    (D) $2\sqrt{3}$
    (E) 4

157. A five digit number is to be formed using each of the digits 1, 2, 3, 4, and 5 exactly once. How many such numbers are there in which the digits 1 and 2 are next to each other?

    (A) 36
    (B) 48
    (C) 60
    (D) 72
    (E) 120

192

158. Let a, b and c be numbers with $a < b < c$ such that the average of a and b is 4, the average of b and c is 8, and the average of a and c is 6. What is the average of a, b and c?

159. The average (arithmetic mean) salary of employees at a bank with A employees in thousands of dollars is 55, and the average salary of employees at a bank with B employees in thousands of dollars is 95. When the salaries of both banks are combined, the average salary in thousands of dollars is 71. What is the value of $\dfrac{A}{B}$?

160. How many integers between 5000 and 8000 have digits that are all different and that increase from left to right?

ANSWERS TO SUPPLEMENTAL PROBLEMS

LEVEL 1: NUMBER THEORY

1. E
2. B
3. D
4. A
5. C
6. 81
7. 9.2
8. 202

LEVEL 1: ALGEBRA AND FUNCTIONS

9. C
10. D
11. A
12. E
13. A
14. 4/3 or 1.33
15. 5/3, 1.66 or 1.67
16. 11

LEVEL 1: GEOMETRY

17. D
18. A
19. D
20. 28
21. 74
22. 92
23. 16
24. 50

LEVEL 1: PROBABILITY AND STATISTICS

25. E
26. A
27. C
28. 2/17, .117, or .118
29. 28
30. 537
31. 16
32. 25

LEVEL 2: NUMBER THEORY

33. A
34. B
35. E
36. C
37. D
38. 35
39. 24
40. 18

LEVEL 2: ALGEBRA AND FUNCTIONS

41. C
42. D
43. A
44. B
45. B
46. 10
47. 4
48. 44

LEVEL 2: GEOMETRY

49. A
50. C
51. D
52. B
53. C
54. 34
55. 6
56. 360

LEVEL 2: PROBABILITY AND STATISTICS

57. E
58. B
59. C
60. C
61. 72
62. 22
63. 11
64. 16

LEVEL 3: NUMBER THEORY

65. E
66. C
67. D
68. D
69. 6
70. 105
71. 20
72. 1024

LEVEL 3: ALGEBRA AND FUNCTIONS

73. B
74. E
75. E
76. C
77. E
78. E
79. 625
80. 1

LEVEL 3: GEOMETRY

81. D
82. D
83. B
84. B
85. 3.2
86. 62.5
87. 6
88. 100

LEVEL 3: PROBABILITY AND STATISTICS

89. D
90. A
91. D
92. 11
93. 3
94. 1/2 or .5
95. 720
96. 11

LEVEL 4: NUMBER THEORY

97. E
98. C
99. C
100. B
101. A
102. E
103. 1
104. 96

LEVEL 4: ALGEBRA AND FUNCTIONS

105. D
106. E
107. B
108. 12
109. 8
110. 3
111. 21
112. 64

LEVEL 4: GEOMETRY

113. E
114. E
115. A
116. 45/2 or 22.5
117. 18
118. 57.8
119. 4
120. 32

LEVEL 4: PROBABILITY AND STATISTICS

121. C
122. E
123. D
124. C
125. 120
126. 56
127. 27
128. 45

LEVEL 5: NUMBER THEORY

129. B
130. A
131. E
132. D
133. E
134. 38
135. 33
136. 5

LEVEL 5: ALGEBRA AND FUNCTIONS

137. D
138. C
139. E
140. B
141. C
142. 23
143. 12.3
144. 12

Level 5: Geometry

145. C
146. C
147. E
148. A
149. A
150. 20
151. 17/4 or 4.25
152. 11.1, 11.2, 11.3, 11.4 , 11.5, 11.6, 11.7, 11.8, or 11.9

Level 5: Probability and Statistics

153. E
154. C
155. D
156. A
157. B
158. 6
159. 3/2 or 1.5
160. 5

YOUR ROAD
TO SUCCESS

$\mathcal{C}$ongratulations! By practicing the problems in this book you have given yourself a significant boost to your SAT math score. Go ahead and take a practice SAT. The math score you get should be much higher than the score you received on your PSAT.

What should you do to get your score even higher? Good news! You can use this book over and over again to continue to increase your score – right up to an 800. All you need to do is change the problems you are focusing on.

If you are currently scoring less than a 400 you should go back and focus on those Level 1 problems.

If you are between a 400 and 500 you should focus on Level 2 problems, but do all the Level 1 problems and some Level 3 problems as well.

If you are between a 500 and 600, then focus on Level 2 and 3 problems, and throw in a few Level 4 problems every now and then.

If you are between a 600 and 700, then the Level 4 problems are really important. Go ahead and work on all of them, but do some Level 2 and 3 problems as well.

Finally, if you are scoring in the 700s, it is time to focus primarily on Level 4 and 5 problems.

These are just general guidelines, and you may want to fine tune this a bit by analyzing each of the four subject areas separately. For example, if you are scoring between a 600 and 700 but you are not getting any Level 4 Geometry problems correct, then shift your focus to Level 3 Geometry problems for a little while. Come back to the Level 4 problems after you become a bit more proficient in Level 3 Geometry.

Similarly, if you are breezing through the Level 4 Number Theory Problems, then start focusing on Level 5 Number Theory. On your next practice test you can try those last few Number Theory questions at the end of each math section.

Upon your next reading, try to solve each problem that you attempt in up to four different ways

- Using an SAT specific math strategy.
- The quickest way you can think of.
- The way you would do it in school.
- The easiest way for you.

Remember – the actual answer is not very important. What is important is to learn as many techniques as possible. This is the best way to simultaneously increase your current score, and increase your level of mathematical maturity.

Keep doing problems from this book for ten to twenty minutes each day right up until two days before your SAT. Mark off the ones you get wrong and attempt them over and over again each week until you can get them right on your own.

I really want to thank you for putting your trust in me and my materials, and I want to assure you that you have made excellent use of your time by studying with this book. I wish you the best of luck on the SAT, on getting into your choice college, and in life.

Steve Warner, Ph.D.
steve@SATPrepGet800.com

ACTIONS TO COMPLETE AFTER YOU HAVE READ THIS BOOK

1. Take another practice SAT

You should see a substantial improvement in your score.

2. Continue to practice SAT math problems for 10 to 20 minutes each day

Keep practicing problems of the appropriate levels until two days before the SAT. For additional practice use *The 32 Most Effective SAT Math Strategies*.

3. Use my Forum page for additional help

If you feel you need extra help that you cannot get from this book, please feel free to post your questions in my new forum at www.satprepget800.com/forum.

4. Review this book

If this book helped you, please post your positive feedback on the site you purchased it from; e.g. Amazon, Barnes and Noble, etc.

5. Claim your FREE bonuses

If you have not done so yet, visit the following webpage and enter your email address to receive an electronic copy of the *SAT Prep Official Study Guide Math Companion*, and solutions to all the supplemental problems in this book.

www.thesatmathprep.com/320SATprmT1.html

About the Author

Steve Warner, a New York native, earned his Ph.D. at Rutgers University in Pure Mathematics in May, 2001. While a graduate student, Dr. Warner won the TA Teaching Excellence Award.

After Rutgers, Dr. Warner joined the Penn State Mathematics Department as an Assistant Professor. In September, 2002, Dr. Warner returned to New York to accept an Assistant Professor position at Hofstra University. By September 2007, Dr. Warner had received tenure and was promoted to Associate Professor. He has taught undergraduate and graduate courses in Precalculus, Calculus, Linear Algebra, Differential Equations, Mathematical Logic, Set Theory and Abstract Algebra.

Over that time, Dr. Warner participated in a five year NSF grant, "The MSTP Project," to study and improve mathematics and science curriculum in poorly performing junior high schools. He also published several articles in scholarly journals, specifically on Mathematical Logic.

Dr. Warner has over 15 years of experience in general math tutoring and over 10 years of experience in SAT math tutoring. He has tutored students both individually and in group settings.

In February, 2010 Dr. Warner released his first SAT prep book "The 32 Most Effective SAT Math Strategies." The second edition of this book was released in January, 2011.

Currently Dr. Warner lives in Staten Island with his two cats, Achilles and Odin. Since the age of 4, Dr. Warner has enjoyed playing the piano—especially compositions of Chopin as well as writing his own music. He also maintains his physical fitness through weightlifting.

BOOKS BY DR. STEVE WARNER

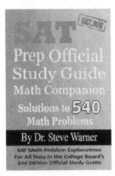

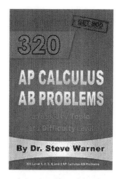

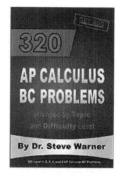

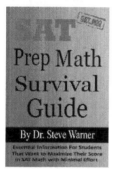

Made in the USA
Lexington, KY
22 June 2015